BAILLIE SCOTT

to Alison · Christmas '95

BAILLIE SCOTT

THE ARTISTIC HOUSE

by Diane Haigh

AD ACADEMY EDITIONS

Acknowledgements

No one can study the work of M.H. Baillie Scott without reference to J.D. Kornwolf's encyclopedic monograph of 1972, which first set out the locational sequence of his buildings and the dates of his published articles and personal records. Though indebted to Kornwolf's work, this book does not seek to replicate it. The focus here is quite different: by going back directly to the surviving houses, I have attempted to capture the core of Baillie Scott's creative intentions and achievements. The architect's writings are expressive in themselves, but infinitely stronger when coupled with his buildings. The photographs in this publication – most of them specially commissioned – communicate the architectural qualities which excited Baillie Scott's contemporaries, and still have the power to engage us today, fifty years after his death.

This venture would not have been possible without the kind co-operation of all those who have allowed me to visit their Baillie Scott homes. This book illustrates only a few of those houses, focusing on case studies which represent the development and range of the work, or retain most of their original features and atmosphere. However, every visit has been instructive and I am grateful to everyone for their hospitality and their shared enthusiasm. I would like to thank in particular Mr and Mrs Michael Wallis, Mr and Mrs Michael Allen, and Michael Nedo, for commissioning me to undertake architectural work which has given me an inside-view of Baillie Scott's construction.

This study has been supported by the Architecture Unit of the Arts Council of Great Britain, which first gave me a grant in 1992 to research the possibilities of making an exhibition of the work of Baillie Scott. I am most grateful for the continuing support of the Arts Council, and for the encouragement of the Architecture Unit's Director, Rory Coonan. A grant from the Marc Fitch Foundation also enabled us to proceed with the photography of the houses.

The exhibition which accompanies this publication is a joint venture with Kettle's Yard Gallery, Cambridge. Michael Harrison, the Director of the Gallery, has been involved in each stage of shaping its approach and making it happen.

Both the exhibition and the publication are based on the excellent photographs of Charlotte Wood, without whose insight, enthusiasm and unflagging energies the whole enterprise could not have been realised.

Many other individuals have helped along the way. Some had specific knowledge of Baillie Scott – James Kennedy-Hawkes, for example, was an articled pupil in the Baillie Scott and Beresford office. John Brandon Jones shared his unrivalled experience of the architectural world of the Arts and Crafts architects and kindly lent the only surviving watercolours by Baillie Scott that have come to light. Conversations on specific aspects of the work have also been crucial to my understanding: my thanks to Jane Brown, Nicholas Bullock, Olive Cook, Mark Girouard, Birkin Haward, Dean Hawkes, Simon Houfe, Peter Kelly, Jill Lever, Mervyn Miller, Margaret Richardson, Peyton Skipwith and Clive Wainwright.

My colleagues and students at Cambridge University Department of Architecture have been endlessly helpful in providing advice, resources and practical assistance. I would like to thank in particular Elizabeth Haylett and Tom Miller, who undertook the task of doing the drawings for publication.

This project has been a long enterprise for me, truly a labour of love, and my family has given me their enthusiasm and support. This book is dedicated to them – William, Eleanor and Francis Fawcett – with love and gratitude.

Cover: Exterior detail of Church Rate Corner, Cambridge, 1924
Page 2: Inside a Baillie Scott house: view through the front door of 48 Storey's Way, Cambridge, 1913

Unless otherwise indicated, all house photographs are by Charlotte Wood.

First published in Great Britain in 1995 by
ACADEMY EDITIONS
An imprint of the

ACADEMY GROUP LTD
42 Leinster Gardens London W2 3AN
Member of the VCH Publishing Group

ISBN: 1 85490 432 9

Distributed to the trade in the USA by
NATIONAL BOOK NETWORK INC
4720 Boston Way, Lanham, Maryland 20706

Printed and bound in the United Kingdom

Contents

Introduction

The ideal of the artistic house promised grace and sanctuary in late-nineteenth-century England. Within the context of the Arts and Crafts movement, it had specific connotations: 'Plans and elevations became the expression of utility; a building's materials were taken from its locality, being cheaper and in harmony with its surroundings. Details were taken from vernacular originals and the architects were interested in craft and in employing plasterers, painters and carvers to enrich their buildings. Ornament was based on nature.'[1] M.H. Baillie Scott worked in this context and shared these ideals, but his was a lone and different voice. He had no part in the movement as it existed in London. He did not train in an Arts and Crafts practice, and did not belong to the emerging 'clubs' of the Art-Worker's Guild or the S.P.A.B.[2] He never met Morris, nor heard Webb speak. In contrast, he started his career in isolation on the Isle of Man. His approach developed independently, and produced fresh propositions.

Baillie Scott's specific interest was in the smaller house. He was deeply critical of the long rows of terraces which were then eating up the countryside in an era of unprecedented suburban growth, for he felt their accommodation was cramped and pretentious, misconceived as a 'mansion in miniature'. His alternative was, in true Arts and Crafts style, based on the cottage – but out of this prototype he developed a wholly new concept for a house of comfort, economy and beauty.

For Baillie Scott, house and garden were a continuum: the house found a niche within a structure of sheltered outdoor spaces covering the whole site, whilst the garden was conceived as an extension of the house-spaces, addressed from inside. In his work domestic interiors gained a new sense of space and light. Ornamentation with patterns based on natural forms was an early enthusiasm, in line with established Arts and Crafts ideals: the interiors of Baillie Scott's first houses of the 1890s were decorated with intense craftsmanship and glowing colours. However, he came to realise that the materials of the buildings could themselves be worked to provide a texture of surface, without additional decoration. 'The artistic house is based on the very essence of its structure, not on frillings and adornments', he wrote in his influential book, *Houses and Gardens* (1906). Baillie Scott sought to draw out the inherent beauty and special character of each material. Inspired by the 'old art of building', he created houses of simplicity and poetry.

As a person Baillie Scott remains elusive, his personal reticence compounded by the destruction of his drawings in two disastrous fires. This study revisits the rich record of the work that remains to be found in the form of his many surviving built works and published writings. It seeks to recapture his powerful vision of the poetry to be wrought in building, and to illustrate afresh his carefully nurtured, and still relevant, achievement.

Notes

1. Margaret Richardson, *Architects of the Arts and Crafts Movement*, Trefoil, London 1983.
2. S.P.A.B., the 'Society for the Protection of Ancient Buildings', dubbed 'Anti-Scrape', was founded in 1877 by William Morris.

OPPOSITE: Blackwell, Windemere, Westmorland, 1898 from fields above the lake.

The Emergence of an Arts and Crafts Architect

EDUCATION

In late Victorian England the quality of an architect's education was very uncertain. Many of Baillie Scott's contemporaries had little schooling outside their profession: Lethaby (b. 1857) left Barnstaple Grammar School to become an articled pupil at the age of fourteen; Voysey (b. 1857) went briefly to Dulwich College before being articled at seventeen; Lutyens (b. 1869) was taught at home and started training at the age of fifteen – at twenty he was in practice. But Baillie Scott came from an affluent family and received a full school education before embarking on his professional career. His learning is evident in the forcefulness of his writing and the scope of his references.

From 1886 to 1889 Baillie Scott was articled to Major Charles E. Davis, City Architect of Bath – and an unlikely master for a pupil with Arts and Crafts sympathies. At this time Davis was 'restoring' the Roman baths in order to construct the new Queen's Bath and Pump Room. Pevsner wrote dismissively of the project: 'The weak south end of the colonnade is by C.E. Davis.' A later work, the Empire Hotel, came in for harsher criticism: 'an unbelievable piece of *pompier* architecture… in the roof there are side by side a large Loire-style gable and two small Norman-Shavian tile-hung gables. The Avon front is in the same frolicsome spirit. What can have gone on in the mind of the designing architect?'[1]

Baillie Scott appears to have spent most of his apprenticeship surveying tessellated Roman pavements, experience that could have prepared him for little in his career – unless it engendered the pattern-making skills which flowered so splendidly later. While working for Davis, however, he lodged at the home of a builder and mason, and this may have brought him more fruitful contacts with the world of building tradesmen. On his application form for membership of the Royal Institute of British Architects many years later, he stated that he had experience in the workshops of various trades, without saying when it was acquired: it may have been during this period in Bath.

Perhaps as important a foundation was his earlier training at the Royal Agricultural College in Cirencester, from 1883 to 1885. Baillie Scott's family owned sheep ranches in Australia and he, as the eldest son, was groomed to run them. He completed his agricultural training, graduating with a Silver Medal, but at the last moment decided to capitalise on his boyhood interest in art and become an architect instead. The exact circumstances of this change of heart are unclear: he later jested that he had been inspired to stay by his first experience of a Gilbert and Sullivan opera in London. Whatever his real reasons, he retained from this period the air of a countryman, as John Betjeman recalled, and acquired practical knowledge that was put to good use.

Baillie Scott told Betjeman another implausible tale to explain why he settled on the Isle of Man after going there on his wedding trip with Florence Nash in 1889. He claimed that he had been so sea-sick on the voyage over that he could not contemplate the trip back. A more likely reason for staying was ambition – specifically the prospect of designing the houses marked on a grand development plan for Onchan. He found employment with the originator of the plan, a surveyor called Fred Saunderson, and, although the plan was never realised, remained with him for three years until he set up his own practice in 1892.

FROM ABOVE: Carved corbel portrait of Baillie Scott aged about twenty-eight, from a series at Ivydene, Douglas, 1893; An example of inspiration taken from publication: Ernest George's published design for a house on Streatham Common … and Baillie Scott's house for Mr MacAndrew, Douglas, 1893.
OPPOSITE: An early hall-house: Five Gables, Cambridge, 1897–8. Double doors opening on to central living room.

The Dream of John Ball

The Arts and Crafts movement can be seen as a direct descendant of the Gothic Revival, which rejected the 'false manifestations' in all spheres of nineteenth-century life – religion, commerce, manners, education, literature, and of course architecture – and turned to the medieval world for inspiration. In architecture, the Gothic Revival is linked to two names above all: its most influential practitioner, A.W.N. Pugin (1812–1852), and its main polemicist, John Ruskin (1819–1900). Baillie Scott's partner Beresford said, even as late as 1945, that he always tried to include a quotation from Ruskin in everything he wrote. Ruskin stoked up the movement's hostility to anything connected with the classical tradition: 'Instant degradation followed [Renaissance architecture] in every direction – a flood of folly and hypocrisy.'[2] But, more importantly, he introduced the immensely powerful notion that good art flows from the craftsmen who create it. That, Ruskin believed, was the 'secret' of Gothic art. William Morris (1834–1896) went to Oxford as a student in 1853, discovered Ruskin, and devoted his life to making the world more Ruskinian – by word and even more by example.

In 1859 Morris built the Red House, an attempt to adapt late Gothic methods of building to nineteenth-century needs. The architect was his friend Philip Webb, whom he had met in the office of George Edmund Street during an abortive architectural training. Two years later, in 1861, he started the firm Morris, Marshall, Faulkner & Co. (later plain Morris & Co.) to produce handcrafted decorative arts: stained glass, furniture, printed

FROM ABOVE: Window in screen at Ivydene, Douglas, 1893; Dining room window at Red House, Douglas, 1893. RIGHT: Hall at stairs in Morris's Red House, Bexley Heath, designed by Philip Webb in 1859.

fabrics and wallpapers. Morris established the unity of 'high' art and 'humble' crafts, and the next generation embraced the idea as an article of faith. Mackmurdo (1851–1942) founded the Century Guild of artist-craftsmen in 1883, the Art-Worker's Guild formed in 1884, and Ashbee (1863–1942) set up the Guild of Handicraft in 1888.

This was the artistic world which Baillie Scott entered at his most impressionable age. He seems to have responded to these ideas wholeheartedly, but as an outsider. He never worked in one of the key practices; he had no exposure to the hothouse atmosphere of London circles. His professional status was entirely conventional, in contrast to some of his contemporaries. Ernest Gimson and the Barnsley brothers, for example, were given Morris's personal blessing: they entered the most prestigious offices as pupils, spent a few years at the centre of the London architectural world – and then retreated to rural Gloucestershire, where they remained the rest of their lives, producing furniture and only a few handcrafted buildings.

However, the Arts and Crafts movement was much more than an aesthetic fin-de-siècle fashion: it was a complete world-view, a vision of a better state of things. Morris made the most complete presentation of that new world in his two Utopian novels, *The Dream of John Ball* (1888) and *News from Nowhere* (1891). Whilst Baillie Scott did not appear to embrace Morris's socialism, he learned from him the fundamental values of the artist-craftsman, and devoted the whole of his long working life to translating the word-pictures of Morris into architectural form.

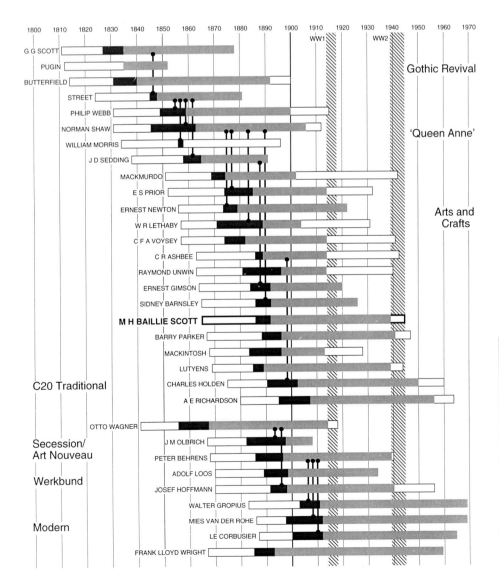

ABOVE: Daneway House, Sapperton, Gloucestershire, home of the Arts and Crafts designer Sidney Barnsley. LEFT: Genealogy of the architects of the Arts and Crafts movement.

THE ISLE OF MAN

Out of this curiously mixed educational background, Baillie Scott emerged a skilful, imaginative Arts and Crafts designer. His talent was fed by a number of distinct sources of inspiration – most notably the 'old work' he had sketched during his childhood in Sussex and his student years around the Cotswolds, and the traditional architecture of the farms and villages he had encountered during his agricultural training. The catalogues of the Fine Art and Industrial Guild of the Isle of Man show that throughout the 1890s he was exhibiting watercolours and pastel studies with titles such as 'The Old Town, Hastings', 'Elizabethan Country House', and 'Lane near Bath', in addition to his own designs.

Clearly Baillie Scott was also aware of contemporary practice. During his training in Bath he would have had access to journals such as *The Architect* and *Building News,* which published houses by the older generation of architects. His first houses on the Isle of Man echo the half-timbered vocabulary of the much-published domestic work of Ernest George and George Devey. J.D. Kornwolf argues that Baillie Scott must also have known the Shingle Style through publications such as the *American Architect.*[3] But American publications must have been hard to come by, and it is perhaps more likely that he was introduced to American developments by a fellow architect on the Isle of Man, Armitage Rigby, who had visited the United States on a study tour.

Even with such access to information, the Isle of Man provided Baillie Scott with some years of relative isolation, allowing him to develop his own ideas independently. He took classes in watercolour and geometry at Douglas School of Art, where he met Archibald Knox (1864–1933), a Manx artist-designer whose work drew on the revival of interest in the island's history and archaeology, in particular its Celtic traditions of art. Knox traced the spiralling tracery on Celtic crosses and jewellery and wove these forms into his own designs, particularly for metalwork. Baillie Scott's friendship with Knox undoubtedly made him more aware of characteristically Northern cultural traditions. The influence of Celtic patterns might be seen, for example, in the doors to his Castletown Police Station, which incorporate decorative spiralling metalwork. The influence of form is also evident: the building's location next to Greeba Castle provoked Baillie Scott to echo the roundness of the castle keep with his own pepperpot tower on the opposite corner.

Baillie Scott buildings on the Isle of Man.
FROM ABOVE: Castletown Police Station, 1900. The tower with a pepperpot roof responds to the corner keep of Greeba Castle on the opposite corner; Ivydene, Little Switzerland, 1893, staircase. Internally the detailing derives from Jacobean sources as used by Shaw or Sedding.
LEFT: Externally, Ivydene's timber framing and carved gables echo the old Cheshire farmhouses beloved by Baillie Scott.
OPPOSITE: Stone gable of Castletown Police Station.

THE RED HOUSE, 1892–3

Baillie Scott started his practice on the Isle of Man in confident style by building a house for his own family. This still stands in wonderful condition, and is even now a place of extraordinary intensity and vitality. The foundation stone was laid by Baillie Scott's seventeen-month-old son on the 20th of October 1892, when the architect himself was only three days away from his twenty-seventh birthday.

As Baillie Scott's first major work, the Red House is full of quotations from other sources. Based in the world of the romantic imagination, it echoes both the medieval spirit and the name of William Morris's own first home. The materials used on the exterior – red brick and tile-hanging – are not indigenous to the Isle of Man and had to be imported. They are combined with the timberwork of Cheshire farmhouses, carved into elaborate patterns on the barge boards and lintels. The overtly medieval decoration is carried through into the interior in carved grotesques and friezes.

This rather naive medievalism is coupled with an important innovation – the opening up of internal space. At the Red House Baillie Scott began to explore the possibilities of opening living rooms into one another. The three main rooms are separated only by screens: when the screens are in place, they contain doors; when they are moved to planned positions, they open up the centre of the house, turning it into a single space. This astonishing transformation is still entirely practical: the current owners tend to alternate between open and closed modes depending on the season or the size of the gathering in the house.

Baillie Scott never built another new home for himself, but renovated at least three old houses. However, he did make a design for a 'House for an Architect' in 1901 which shows an even bolder openness of space, only this time with a separate office – a lesson learned from living and working in the Red House.

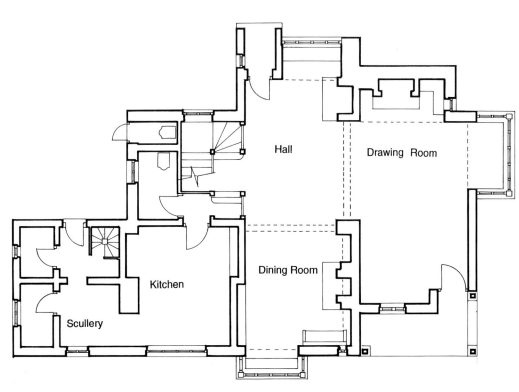

The Red House was Baillie Scott's first experiment in opening up the house plan.
FROM ABOVE: The hall enclosed with screens in place; Screens removed to create a continuum of ground-floor rooms; Baillie Scott seated in the hall ingle (from Dekorative Kunst, *vol. 5, 1900).*
Morris's description of the hostel parlour in The Dream of John Ball *could have been taken directly from a Baillie Scott interior: 'The walls were panelled roughly enough with oak boards to about six foot from the floor, and about three foot of plaster above that was wrought in a pattern of rose stem running all round the room, freely and roughly done but with wonderful skill and spirit. On the hood of the great chimney was a huge rose wrought in plaster. A quaintly carved sideboard held an array of bright pewter pots and dishes and wooden and earthen bowls; a stout oak table went up and down the room and a carved oak chair stood by the chimney-corner... That, except for the rough stools, was all the furniture.'*
LEFT: Ground-floor plan.
OPPOSITE: Detail of the drawing room fireplace, which glows with medieval intensity.

'OLD WORK'

The spirit of 'old work' is the touchstone which runs through Baillie Scott's architecture, and the key to understanding it. Baillie Scott found inspiration in the spaces and textures of fine old manor houses and attempted to integrate these qualities into new domestic building. Misinterpreted, this admiration has been the reason for dismissing his work as merely sentimental.

William Morris himself admired English vernacular buildings. He left his Red House in Bexley Heath in 1865, and from 1871 leased Kelmscott Manor, a sixteenth-century Cotswold stone manor house in Oxfordshire. The move symbolised a change of heart. He now saw the rural vernacular as the way forward, and wrote of his hope 'that it will be from such unnecessary, unpretentious buildings that the new and genuine architecture will spring, rather than our experiments in conscious style'. Morris's later Utopian novels described a rural life far from the oppression of late-nineteenth-century industrial cities, which allowed men and women to be free and fulfilled. His romantic vision opened the eyes of the succeeding generation, among them Baillie Scott.

In the years between his first family house and his first published articles of 1895, Baillie Scott moved away from a derivative approach to past work. He no longer drew eclectically on different styles but began to use direct observation of vernacular buildings, particularly those of the sixteenth and seventeenth centuries: timber-framed Cheshire and Shropshire farmhouses, Sussex cottages and Cotswold stone manor houses. At that time many of these buildings would still have been in daily use, unsanitised by restoration – their worn and gentle fabric a rebuke to the mechanical perfection and loud coloration of then-new Victorian buildings.

The central issue for Arts and Crafts architects who sought to transcend stylistic copying was the vitality of craftsmanship. In old buildings they saw not only an excellence of technique but also a wealth of inventiveness and creativity in every detail. Baillie Scott wrote: 'In "old work" we chiefly consider a certain aesthetic rightness and beauty expressed in practical ways. It is not until we get back to the work of the earlier builders that our hearts are touched and thrilled by the strange charm of the building art as then practised.' This was not mere nostalgia, but evidence of a vital principle which could make the world a better place: 'to repudiate all this heritage of beautiful work seems as unreasonable as to attempt to produce lifeless and mechanical copies of it'.

While some of his generation, such as Ashbee, Gimson and the Barnsley brothers, decided to become craftsmen-designers and took up a craft, Baillie Scott always saw his role firmly as a designer. He allowed local craftsmen – blacksmiths, plasterers, bricklayers, carpenters – to draw out the qualities of their materials to his specification. And he built in the traditions of each locality: stonework in the Cotswolds, pargetted plasterwork in Essex, roughcast in the Lake District, tile-hanging in Kent. Though he sought simplicity and directness above all, his approach, like the 'old work', delighted in unexpected details: the insertion of a little window, the addition of an adornment to celebrate the moment, the opening up of a view.

Examples of the kind of 'old work' so admired by Baillie Scott. Photos by Edwin Smith.
FROM ABOVE: Pattenden Manor, Goudhurst, Kent; House at Ainstock, Oxfordshire.
OPPOSITE: Mrs Clarke's house, Lindfield, Sussex.

PUBLICATION

Architectural publications had a profound impact on the development of Baillie Scott's career. They put him in touch with the larger issues debated by his peers, and allowed him to see new projects that were too far away from the Isle of Man to visit in person. In turn, he was assiduous in promoting his own projects. Even his first inept, unbuilt design was submitted to the *Building News* and duly published in 1890. No doubt this early success encouraged his enthusiasm for publication. Most of his built projects appeared both as design drawings and as photographs of completed works. In addition he illustrated his ideas through a series of imaginary schemes with descriptive names such as 'Trevista' for a house organised on three axes, 'Trecourt' for a house planned around a courtyard, and 'Yellowsands' for a holiday home. Baillie Scott's name and work recur frequently in the architectural magazines of the time. The list of his publications in Kornwolf's monograph is extensive, marking an energetic campaign which continued throughout his working life.

Of particular importance was *The Studio,* a new magazine which aspired to be 'at once the rallying-point and the radical centre of the new movement in the modern arts'. From the very start, Baillie Scott must have seen in it an articulation of his own aspirations. Its first issue in April 1893 declared its firm support of 'every fresh and honest effort to get away from the curse of plagiarism in domestic architecture'. One article, 'Artistic Houses', showed the latest, heavily decorated interiors by Morris & Co. – but the editor pointed out that ideas on interiors were changing, and praised C. F. A. Voysey for the 'studied simplicity of his work, his reliance for effect on the simplicity of proportion, [and] his delight in broad unrelieved surfaces'. A second article contained an interview with Voysey himself. By Volume Four, Baillie Scott had become one of a small handful of architect contributors to *The Studio*. Through this publication, his work reached a wide readership in England and Europe, gaining him both sympathetic readers and commissions far beyond his island home.

The central theme of his articles during this period remained fairly constant: the choice between the kind of houses then being built in endless suburban terraces, and his approach, which he defined as preferable in every respect. He poured scorn on the 'glaring defects' of conventional houses: 'the doll's-house-like prettiness of the so-called Queen Anne bijou residence has been held to be as undesirable on the one hand as the stolid ugliness of the commoner box of bricks of the suburban house on the other'. He objected to their materials, their construction, their planning: the materials were harsh and refused to mellow; the construction was untrue, as in 'half-timber work constructed of inch planks nailed on the brick wall'; the plans were merely shrunken versions of a mansion, reduced until 'the minimum of size and the maximum of discomfort are reached – a small room which is already filled to overflowing with unnecessary and incongruous furniture'. But most odious of all, in his list of hates, was the 'smirking pretentiousness' of the houses.

Baillie Scott would follow his barrage of invective by outlining his calmer vision of the ideal suburban house, an economical alternative within reach of the average householder 'of moderate means', but appealing, more specifically, to the man who had achieved 'some cultivation, some love of the beautiful in his surroundings'.

Baillie Scott's published drawings of 'A Small Country House', from The Studio, *December 1897.*
FROM ABOVE: View of house from southeast; Staircase; Central hall.

A Small Country House: Five Gables, Cambridge, 1897–8

In several instances the publication of an article in *The Studio* gave rise to a commission. In the December 1897 issue Baillie Scott discussed the particular problems of organising the small house, providing a sample plan and sketches to illustrate his ideas. This paper scheme was realised the next year in a house called Five Gables in Cambridge. The close correspondence between the building and the article gives a clear indication of the practicality of Baillie Scott's theories at this time.

The plan of Five Gables revolves around the central hall with its corner fireplace. The generosity of this area adds immeasurably to the sense of spaciousness in the small house, in contrast with the narrow hallway found in the average terrace of the period. The hall is bright, drawing in light from down the stairs and through the window opposite, with its built-in window seat. Most importantly, it opens directly into the drawing room and dining room through elegant double doors containing glass roundels. Thus, whilst the hall's role as the hub of circulation compromises its use as a sitting room, it can be transformed, as at the Red House, into the central element in a continuous ground-floor space.

Nevertheless, the centralised planning raises a number of problems. Significantly, the plans give no indication of orientation or site organisation. When faced with a real, generously proportioned plot, Baillie Scott evidently experienced some confusion about where to put the house. In comparison with later projects, the site organisation is not well resolved: the front door faces east towards the road, two bay windows face south towards the plot boundary, while the best view down the garden is left to the kitchen offices.

The exterior of the building mirrors the published sketches almost exactly. The formal organisation marks a considerable advance on the contortions of the Red House, although it includes similar elements – a suggestion of a Dutch stepped gable on the chimney, and a similar mix of materials – red brick, half-timbering, roughcast. The roof forms are handled with greater ease: the long roof on the east elevation pulls down to cover the ground-floor verandah, whilst the gable on the road elevation plays against another gable half-hidden by the chimney on the south.

Internally, there are further delights in the detailing. *The Studio* article on the project is mainly devoted to the effects to be achieved in spaces of 'repose and restfulness, warmth and lightness. Every detail must be chosen to form part of the original idea.' From the splendid front door right through to the servant's bedroom, the internal hierarchy of the house is mirrored in a whole family of differently detailed doors, most incorporating glazed lights and carefully designed ironmongery. The fireplaces also accord with their situation. The one in the drawing room is flanked by white settles, and has light finials rising to the ceiling, whilst the dining room ingle is entirely occupied by a single long settle lit by a small, shuttered window. As Baillie Scott wrote, 'In the dining room the most striking feature is the inglenook in the corner with its red-brick back, copper hood and its wide brick hearth.' This is a fine piece of fantasy and enjoyment – Baillie Scott at his best.

Not every aspect of this house attains the full stature of Baillie Scott's mature schemes, but it still gives a fascinating glimpse of the development of his work. Already far removed from the medieval heaviness of his earliest houses, it points to a new type of house of spaciousness and delight.

'A Small Country House' realised as Five Gables, Grange Road, Cambridge, 1897–8.
FROM ABOVE: Southwest corner; Staircase; View through double doors of hall to dining room inglenook.

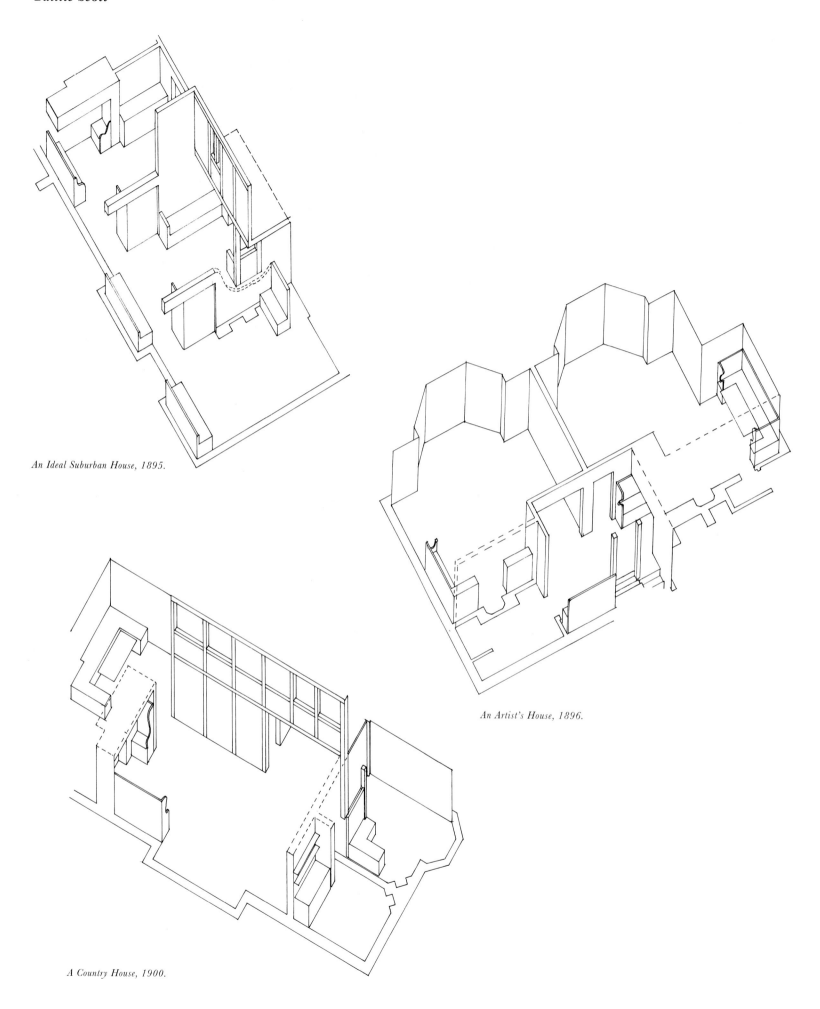

An Ideal Suburban House, 1895.

An Artist's House, 1896.

A Country House, 1900.

IDEAL HOUSES

The full evolution of Baillie Scott's domestic designs can be traced through the series of articles published in *The Studio* during the 1890s. All of the schemes are speculative, although some were subsequently commissioned and built. Their titles are telling: 'An Ideal Suburban Villa', 'An Artist's House' , 'A Small Country House', 'A Country House'. All are essentially smaller houses for artistic clients in a countrified alternative to suburbia. Within this comfortable setting, Baillie Scott developed his revolutionary proposition of open planning.

In each case, Baillie Scott began by leading the reader through the series of internal spaces, relating this experience to the feel of old houses. The relationship between the spaces, and the nature of the volume that contained them, were the critical issues. In his first article in January 1895, Baillie Scott introduced the reader to 'An Ideal Suburban Villa': 'On entering by the front door, we find ourselves in a wide and low porch from which, through an archway to the right, we catch a glimpse of the staircase which rises from a wide corridor leading to the kitchen. It is difficult for me to picture to you the vista-like effect of the broad corridor, but to get some idea of its general effect I must transport you to some old Cheshire farmhouse.' The tour continued into the double-height hall, where a musical evening was in full swing: 'In the ingle, seated on the broad seats, a company of friends are gathered around the blazing wood fire on the wide brick hearth, which lights up the burnished copper of the fire dogs. Above in the gallery are the musicians and the strains of a violin are heard, while the position of the players gives an air of mystery to the music which greatly adds to its effect.'

Behind this romancing lay the development of the hall-house plan. 'An Ideal Suburban Villa' proposes a linear organisation of the principal rooms, with the centre slice formed by a double-height hall which opens through double doors to the rooms on either side. A long view through the spaces is achieved on the south side of the house. This scheme was later built as Bexton Croft in Knutsford, Cheshire.

The proposals for 'An Artist's House' (October 1896) and 'A Small Country House' (December 1897) bring the hall to the entrance side, making it not only the hub of circulation but also a room in its own right, with inglenook fireplace and bay window seat. There are separate living rooms, reached through generous double doors from the hall. Access to the kitchen and servants' quarters is taken out of this central space and marked by a change in level. The main staircase arrives in the hall but is treated as a separate volume. This was the central hall arrangement used in Baillie Scott's own Red House.

In the final, most radical proposal for 'A Country House' (February 1900), a double-height galleried hall dominates the plan of the whole house. The hall is lit by a generous bay window and lined by a series of alcove spaces for the den, bower, children's room and refectory, which are tucked under the upper-floor bedrooms. The sketches show an interplay of small, intimate spaces against the larger volume of the hall. The kitchen offices are set into a separate wing, which forms one side of a courtyard with the front entrance in the inner corner. With this project, the hall-house was transformed into a new proposition – and not just in terms of organisation. The exterior was liberated from historical reference: the only interruptions in the plain white walls and the simple sweep of the roof were the projecting bay windows and the massive rendered chimneys. This was, in Baillie Scott's words, 'in no sense a fancy house, but … a serious attempt to meet the requirements of those who wish to escape from the thralldom of suburban existence'. He included himself in this category as the scheme for his own house, which later reappeared as 'The Crossways', took this most open form.

FROM ABOVE: Double-height hall for the White House, Helensburgh, 1899; Hall and alcove spaces in 'A Country House', 1900.
OPPOSITE: Axonometric projections showing the opening up of interior spaces developed in a series of articles in The Studio, *1895–1900.*

THE BREAKTHROUGH

Somewhere around 1896–7 Baillie Scott's architecture took a great leap out of the heavy half-timbering of his early houses into the broad simplicities of his mature work. Undoubtedly this was the time when he found his direction as an architect.

There has been speculation about the debt that Baillie Scott may have owed to C.F.A. Voysey (1857–1941), whose work was developing along similar paths during the 1890s. Voysey was eight years older and had a very respectable Arts and Crafts pedigree, having worked for the architects Seddon and Devey. He joined the Art-Worker's Guild in 1884 and established himself as a designer of wallpapers and furniture in the 1880s before receiving his first building commissions in the early 1890s.

Voysey's first architectural designs also made use of heavy half-timbering, for example in the upper floors of an unbuilt house designed for himself in 1885, and in the gables of Walnut Tree Farm in 1890. However, by the time of Perrycroft at Malvern (1893) or Lowicks at Frensham, Surrey (1894), he had found the rough-cast forms and broad hipped roofs of Westmorland green slate that were to characterise the whole of his later work. Voysey's early designs were published in the *British Architect* and later in *The Studio*, and Baillie Scott must have seen them. What did he take from Voysey? The work that is closest in feel to a Voysey building is the little village hall at Onchan, Isle of Man (1897), which uses Voysey's typical elements of a long green slate roof over whitewashed buttressed walls. After this project, the architects' styles diverge – as we can see in the houses each designed by Lake Windermere in 1898.

Baillie Scott's Blackwell has a taut wall surface, with flush windows and even stonework surrounds. Repeated gables saw across the south elevation, culminating in the narrow gable of the west elevation, which stands high above the lake. By contrast, Voysey's long, low roof at Moor Crag sprawls down the hillside, encompassing a verandah and service quarters beneath its skirts. Yet on plan Voysey's design is the more regular. He was never interested in open spatial arrangements: the spatial gymnastics of the double-height hall and low ingles in Blackwell were outside his canon.

During the 1890s Baillie Scott designed a series of houses which, although less refined or decorative than Voysey's designs of the period, developed a richer language of rough-cast walls, strong gables, high roofs and tall chimneys. The bold and upright exteriors were the counterpart of elaborately carved and patterned interiors.

Baillie Scott retained his respect for Voysey and in 1908 wrote an article for *The Studio* on 'The Characteristics of Mr C.F.A. Voysey's Architecture'. He described with real appreciation the devotion required to achieve the completeness of Voysey's work, which he saw as 'the application of severely sane, practical and rational ideas to home-making'. Indeed, Baillie Scott may have found Voysey a little too severe and sane, as he himself moved in the direction of a rougher poetry of texture and space. None the less, in the critical period of 1896–7, he may have derived from Voysey the critical impulse that he needed in order to move forward.

Notes

1. Nikolaus Pevsner, *The Buildings of England: North Somerset and Bristol*, Penguin, London 1958.

2. John Ruskin, *The Stones of Venice*, vol. 1, 1851: p. 23.

3. J.D. Kornwolf, *M.H. Baillie Scott and the Arts and Crafts Movement*, Johns Hopkins Press, Baltimore and London 1972: p. 85.

FROM ABOVE: Village Hall, Onchan, 1897; South front, Blackwell, Westmorland, 1898. OPPOSITE: Garden front of White Lodge, St Mary's Convent, Wantage, Berkshire, 1899.

The Northern Poet

THE ROOM AS A WORK OF ART

As a designer Baillie Scott led a double life. Whilst his writings and the main stream of his architecture developed the simple and spacious interiors of the artistic house, he also completed a series of important commissions for elaborate and highly decorative *Gesamtkunstwerke*, in which he designed not only the spaces but each element in them, including furniture, fabrics, stained glass, rugs and light fittings. It was for these works that he was most widely known during the 1890s, particularly in Europe. Although his interiors still seem to have something of the elaborate heaviness of Norman Shaw's interiors for his own house, or the highly decorated work of Morris & Co., Baillie Scott strove for simplification, and in so doing made an important contribution to the beginnings of the Arts and Crafts movement in Germany. His work was eagerly reviewed in German magazines, and Wasmuth published a German edition of his *Houses and Gardens* in 1912. He continued to receive commissions for work in Austria, Germany and Switzerland until the outbreak of war in 1914.

In these turn-of-the-century years, the architect Hermann Muthesius (1867–1927) served as cultural attaché to the German embassy in London. He was charged with preparing reports on a wide range of buildings and industrial installations, but the real focus of his work – and his real passion – was the English house. His research was published first in a number of articles in magazines such as *Dekorative Kunst*, and then in an unrivalled three-volume survey, *Das Englische Haus* (1904). Muthesius identified William Morris as the key figure who had prepared the way for the Arts and Crafts movement by reintroducing handworking skills 'with the intelligence of explorers and pathfinders'. And he saw in Baillie Scott an artist with a distinctly Northern sensibility: '[With this work] we seem already to have stepped into the world of fantasy and romance of the ancient bardic poetry that was once supposed to have been the legacy of the misty figure of Ossian… With Baillie Scott we are among the purely Northern poets among British architects.'[1] Perhaps some notion of a shared Nordic culture lay behind this romantic view.

The other strand that Muthesius detected was folk art, which was then enjoying a revival in many parts of Europe, although not generally in Britain, for the English seemed to find the 'symbols of an older wiser land' not in native traditions but in 'wallpaper and fabric patterns based on hedgerow flowers and foliage … rustic pewter and rural oak'.[2] Muthesius identified the massive pieces of oak furniture in Baillie Scott's early work as peasant-poetry: 'one feels the real scent of the earth, [but] it is mixed with the aroma of blooming meadow flowers from long ago'.

Baillie Scott must have been flattered by Muthesius's admiration, which spread his influence far beyond the Isle of Man. In Finland, for example, we can find copies of his books in the library at Hvitträsk, where Saarinen, Gesellius and Lindgren 'reinvented' the Finnish National Romantic Style.

FROM ABOVE: Fireplace at Glencrutchery House, Douglas, 1897–8. Note the frieze of windblown trees and scattering birds – a particularly acute observation of the windswept Isle of Man. The house has been demolished, but the fireplace is now at the Wolfsonian Foundation, Miami Beach, Florida; Design for the dining room at the Ducal Palace, Darmstadt; Hall in house for Carl St Amory, Bedford, 1895.
OPPOSITE: Capitals of intertwining flowers around the fireplace in the white drawing room, Blackwell, Westmorland, 1898.

HAUS EINES KUNSTFREUNDES

The admiration of Hermann Muthesius undoubtedly helped Baillie Scott to win a pair of prestigious commissions: the redecoration of two rooms in the Darmstadt palace of Grand Duke Ernst Ludwig of Hesse in 1897, followed the next year by a smaller scheme in Romania for the Grand Duke's sister, Crown Princess Marie. Both projects have been destroyed, but Muthesius's writings give some indication of their romantic characteristics.

At the Darmstadt palace, Baillie Scott developed the idea of each room as an individual and complete creation. This was his first opportunity to realise his designs for furniture on any scale: there were several pieces with fittings in repoussé metalwork, as well as light fixtures, chimney hoods, firebaskets and fingerplates. The work was carried out by Ashbee's Guild of Handicraft: Baillie Scott named the craftsmen involved in his articles in *The Studio*, recording 'the keen pleasure to designer and workman' afforded by these pieces. During their visits to Darmstadt, Baillie Scott and Ashbee met the Grand Duke and discussed his plans to establish an artists' colony to encourage the reintegration of art and craftwork in Hesse – a scheme that was carried out in 1899 with Olbrich and Behrens as its resident architects.

The second project, 'Le Nid', was a tree-house, a place where the Crown Princess could retreat from the formalities of court life. In this fantasy world, each room was 'lined with jewelled and brilliant colour' and decorated with a different flower. The principal room was the sun-room: here the sunflower adorned all tiles, seats and windows, whilst the ceiling represented an 'attempt to convey something of the effect of glimpses of sky and sun seen through the upper branches of trees'. Off this golden bower was a small oratory decorated with a frieze of lilies superscribed with a Rossetti verse: 'We too will stand before that shrine, Occult, withheld, untrod.' This was truly a mystic setting for a Pre-Raphaelite vision.

Baillie Scott's prize-winning entry for the 1901 Darmstadt *Haus eines Kunstfreundes* (An Art-Lover's House) competition was the last of his elaborately worked interiors. The competition gave him the opportunity to combine nearly all of the ideas that he had developed over the previous decade. The perspectives reveal a summary of details realised in earlier schemes: the timber framing is similar to that in the hall at Blackwell, Westmorland, with carved flowers and birds darting amongst the columns, and the peacock frieze in the dining room is the same as in the White House, Helensburgh. The scheme found favour mainly on account of its interior spaces: the double-height hall in particular was seen as excitingly modern. The jury had more doubts about the external elevations, whose forms were clearly derived from the single tower and gable on the police station in Castletown on the Isle of Man.

The competition brought Baillie Scott further recognition and design commissions for Arts and Crafts exhibitions in Berlin, Mannheim, Dresden and Vienna. Much of his furniture was sold in Europe, and some was made in continental workshops such as the Deutsche Werkstätte at Dresden-Hellerau.

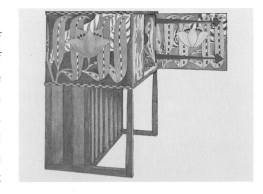

FROM ABOVE: Manx piano painted in the same glowing orange, gold and green colours as the drawing room in the Ducal Palace at Darmstadt, 1897; Central living space of 'Le Nid', a tree-house for the Crown Princess of Romania, 1898. The sunflower colours of the day space contrast with the creamy blue of the lily-lined oratory beyond; Music room of Baillie Scott's prize-winning entry for the Haus eines Kunstfreundes *competition, 1901.*
OPPOSITE: The Haus eines Kunstfreundes *includes many of the features found in Baillie Scott's interiors of the period. Shown from above are:*
The double-height central hallway which opens directly onto various living rooms – note the glimpse of Byzantine detailing in the dining room beyond; Entrance elevation – a collection of pepperpot towers and Castletown gables which found less favour with the jury than the spatial organisation of the interiors.

Blackwell, Westmorland, 1898

Baillie Scott's collaboration with Ashbee on the Darmstadt palace interiors opened his eyes to the full potential of craftwork. His experience is reflected in his subsequent commission for Blackwell, where he designed the furniture, metalwork and fabrics. The house was featured prominently in Muthesius's book, *Das Englische Haus*, and it remains one of the most complete and important interiors of the period. Muthesius drew attention to Baillie Scott's 'new idea of the interior as an autonomous work of art … each room is an individual creation, the elements of which spring from the overall idea'.

The centre of the house is the double-height hall, which in turn is focused on a two-storey 'box-within-a-box' – a deep ingle fireplace with a half-timbered gallery room reached by a winding stair. The main staircase leads to a first-floor gallery with views into the hall and beyond, to the hills outside. At the opposite end of the hall is a single-height billiard room recess with a built-in settle for spectators. This room has carved timber panelling with a glowing peacock frieze – one element not designed by Baillie Scott, but chosen from a catalogue of a range manufactured by Shand Kydd Ltd.

The dining room opens off the hall, and there is a direct visual link between the dining room settle and the hall inglenook. The fireplaces in the two rooms have a strong family resemblance, being composed of interlocking pieces of local stones – green slate and limestone. But the overall feel of the dining room is quite different: its walls have panelling and hessian printed with a flower pattern designed by Baillie Scott.

Blackwell, Westmorland, 1898, was the largest and most elaborate of Baillie Scott's early commissions.
LEFT: Drawing room bay window overlooking Lake Windermere, a view seen right along the passage.
OPPOSITE: Fireplace inglenook in the double-height hall with smoking room above.

The main living rooms face south over rolling lawns. They are linked by a broad and low corridor which terminates in a bay window with a panoramic view of Lake Windermere and the Lakeland hills. Thus the main movement through the house is at right angles, lining up with the lake. The axis ends in the drawing room, an extraordinarily different world of delicate white plasterwork decorated with flowers which are the counterparts of those growing wild on the hillsides – mountain ash, guelder roses, oak and hawthorn. Flower patterns recur in the stained-glass windows that light the fireplaces. The decorative design throughout the house is based on natural forms, abstracted into Byzantine richness.

The exterior of Blackwell shows a remarkable coherence, given that Baillie Scott had previously only tackled much smaller houses. In its materials and forms, it draws on local building traditions: the walls are rough-cast, green slate and sandstone; the profile is defined by tall gables and massive chimneys. However, the scale and formality of the house set it clearly apart from local farmhouses. Here the elements of the vernacular are transformed into a rich and original work – a summation of the Arts and Crafts longing to live in contact with natural beauty.

Blackwell, Westmorland, 1898.
ABOVE: Stained-glass windows in bedroom and drawing room. Note how the varying types of glass and leading contribute to the design.
LEFT: Dining room hessian printed with local wild flowers – rowan, bluebells and daisies.
OPPOSITE: Carved panelling and stone corbel around lower part of hall. The decorative rowan pattern is thought to have been carved by Simpson of Kendal.

FURNITURE CATALOGUE

Baillie Scott's writings return frequently to 'the choice of simple furniture' to create clear, open space in the smaller home. He designed built-in settles, window seats and dressers to eliminate much of the usual clutter, and suggested that any additional pieces had to be in 'absolute harmony with their surroundings', appearing to grow out of the requirements of the room.

Baillie Scott's preference for solid and simple pieces is illustrated by the 1901 catalogue of J. P. White's Pyghtle Works in Bedford, which includes more than eighty of his designs. The catalogue declared: 'The furniture has been designed and made to meet the requirements of those who, appreciating soundness of workmanship and simplicity and reasonableness in design, have not found their wants supplied by the furniture offered to the public in the modern cabinet-maker's shop.' With this furniture, Baillie Scott was appealing to the same people who were the ideal inhabitants of his model Arts and Crafts suburban cottage – people with artistic aspirations but modest incomes.

The Pyghtle Works pieces were not cheap and their rarity suggests that they were not widely sold. Many were illustrated with inlaid decorations of birds or flowers which, it was suggested, might set a theme for a room. But the catalogue also pointed out that 'even reticent ornament' was 'not essential' and that special prices could be given for the simplest treatment of the work. The pieces are straightforward and robust – precursors of Utility furniture. They have neither the elegant exaggeration of Voysey nor the stylistic assertiveness of Mackintosh, but they confirm that Baillie Scott was a furniture designer of great practicality and considerable charm.

FROM ABOVE: Baillie Scott's furniture was presented in the 1901 catalogue of the Pyghtle Works, Bedford. Catalogue cover design by Baillie Scott; Daffodil dresser; Folding table catalogue no. 14 with optional daisy pattern. LEFT: Manx piano case designed in 1896 (courtesy of the Victoria & Albert Museum). OPPOSITE: Daffodil dresser from the 1901 Pyghtle Works catalogue; Table from Onchan Village Hall, 1897

LANDHAUS WALDBÜHL, 1907–11

Waldbühl reveals the scope of Baillie Scott's decorative work when he was supported by a committed and wealthy client. It was commissioned in 1907 by the Swiss industrialist Theodor Bühler (1877–1915), an Anglophile who had spent the first two years of his marriage in Britain and America and had come to see an English country house as the ultimate adjunct to a freer way of life. Bühler had learned about Baillie Scott's work through his book, *Houses and Gardens*, and the accounts of Muthesius. Waldbühl still belongs to the Bühler family, and is the only surviving example of a total Baillie Scott design, encompassing house, interior and garden.

The plan is typical of Baillie Scott's free linear plans of the period, although it is on a larger scale than most. The symmetrical south side is occupied by a series of interconnecting living rooms which relate to the garden through a pair of loggias. The kitchen offices and garage are set in a separate wing, to give an L-shape which encloses two sides of the entrance court. This organisation of space is within the usual bounds of Baillie Scott's work: the interiors, however, go far beyond anything else.

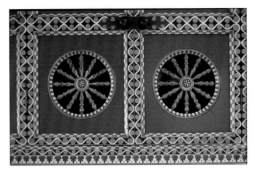

The central hall, dining room and study are lined with timber panels which allude to both English linenfold panelling and traditional Swiss interiors, the latter probably inspired by a book Bühler sent Baillie Scott in 1910. Elements of Swiss folk art can be seen in the carving of the study ceiling, whereas the vine winding round the hall, for example, is a more familiar Baillie Scott motif.

The room least affected by the client's cultural eclecticism is the ladies' drawing room, which is a complete Baillie Scott interior. Here the colours are soft and natural: the walls are covered in a silk fabric with peach-coloured wild roses on a pearly background, the ceiling and frieze are white to accentuate the elaborate plaster patterning. The fireplace is tall, stretching from floor to frieze, but its design is simple, a foil to the complex marking of the materials – pink and green marbles inlaid with mother-of-pearl roundels. Most outstanding of all is the furniture: a settle, armchairs, secrétaire, and a cabinet of black mahogany with inlaid roundel flower patterns in a variety of lighter woods. The forms of the furniture and fireplace are simple and severe: the enjoyment is derived from the grain of the materials and the patterning.

The most abstract piece of furniture is the desk in the study – a simple cubic form with a grid of inlaid ebony strips dividing walnut panels set with a strong diagonal grain. There is no pattern here, except the play of the black grid against the zigzag of the walnut. This piece may have been influenced by Josef Hoffmann's designs for the Palais Stoclet – which were published in *The Studio* in 1906 – but the simplicity of the overall concept was undoubtedly enriched by Baillie Scott's distinct awareness of the patterning inherent in the materials.

The strongest effects are reserved for the children's room, where painted patterning decorates the panelling battens, architraves and doors, and the toy cupboard is painted in pink and orange with white and blue borders. In contrast, the parents' bedroom has a more muted green panelling, with beading and architraves picked out in a pattern of starry white hawthorn blossom. Muthesius said that for Baillie Scott colour was everything: Waldbühl illustrates exactly the strength of coloration that prompted this remark.

Notes

1. Hermann Muthesius, *The English House* (abridged English translation edited by Dennis Sharp), Lund Humphries, London 1979: p. 47.

2. Isabelle Anscombe, *Arts and Crafts Style*, Phaidon, Oxford 1991.

Waldbühl, Uzwil, 1907–11.
FROM ABOVE: Marble fireplace in drawing room;
Painted decoration on the toy cupboard in the children's room; Inlay work on music cabinet.
OPPOSITE, FROM ABOVE L. TO R.: Ladies' drawing room with furniture and fabrics designed by Baillie Scott; Study; Inlaid music cabinet; Detail of inlay work on display cabinet.

Houses and Gardens

·BAILLIE SCOTT·

In 1901 Baillie Scott left the Isle of Man and moved with his family to Bedford. At that time he was winning increasing recognition both in England and abroad, especially in Germany. His prospects for work on the Isle of Man were clearly limited; he also began to suspect the local building contractors of copying his ideas rather than employing him directly. One possible reason for choosing Bedford was that it was the base of J.P. White, the furniture-manufacturer who had just produced a catalogue of his work. Bedford also had a community of like-minded artists and architects: Baillie Scott had designed a house in the town for the musician Carl St Amory in 1893, and the Arts and Crafts architects Griggs and Mallows both practised there.

The years immediately after the move proved difficult. The family found Bedford uncongenial and they soon moved to 'The Manor' at Fenlake, a mile or so outside town. Baillie Scott also found little support for his work, and his commissions declined sharply. It took him until 1905 to re-establish his reputation.

The publication in 1906 of Baillie Scott's book, *Houses and Gardens*, marked the high-point of his career. This was a substantial book of 247 pages – the fruit of a year's preparation – fully illustrated with drawings and watercolours which defined and described his vision of the artistic house. Most of the books on small houses produced during this period were compendiums of designs. In comparison, the originality of Baillie Scott's book shone out. The argument and the answers were all his own.

The first chapters opened the argument, describing Baillie Scott's view of houses as they were – and the promise of what they might be, transformed by his persuasive ideas. Subsequent chapters outlined first the new possibilities for each space in the house, and then the simple but expressive construction required to realise this haven. Baillie Scott's principles of rational planning were not limited to one size of house but could be applied to all types of dwelling, from cottage to apartment block. The final section illustrated thirty schemes, built and unbuilt, to demonstrate how all these ideas could be drawn into practical proposals to suit all budgets and sites, town or country.

Houses and Gardens presented a distinctive vision of a new direction in architecture, with its beguiling images of plain-gabled houses under long, low roofs, extraordinarily spacious halls, and flowering gardens. It was widely read and undoubtedly resulted in many new commissions. Baillie Scott's houses of the 1906–14 period are perhaps his happiest designs – simple and self-assured, but still most enjoyable to inhabit.

HOUSES AS THEY ARE AND AS THEY MIGHT BE

Houses and Gardens developed the ideas of the articles in *The Studio* during the 1890s. Baillie Scott began by attacking the ubiquitous red-brick suburban terrace. He deplored their standard forms, which undermined the diversity of English towns, and their pretentious details, which were added on by speculators to attract sales. He then presented his alternative: 'The house which, for want of a better word, we must continue to differentiate from the ordinary house as artistic, bases its claims not on its frillings and on its adornments, but on the very essence of its structure.' No spurious art, but an honesty of scale, construction and furnishing was the foundation of the work. No element pretended to be something else: this was a 'roomy and commodious cottage, not a mansion in miniature'. Baillie Scott was moving towards design stripped of extraneous detail, which relied – in an extraordinarily modern sense – on the exposed texture of construction. The structure contributed greatly to the beauty of the house, though it was sometimes obscured to meet practical requirements or to supply plain surfaces of pure colour. Baillie Scott declared: 'When in doubt, whitewash might well be taken as a maxim to be followed in the decoration of the modern house' – a radical notion for the beginning of the twentieth century.

The other startling proposition of the artistic house was its spaciousness. Baillie Scott began to work out the plan implications of opening up interiors in the 1890s; in 1900 his radical plan for 'A Country House' described a great hall flanked by recess spaces. His examples of 1906 skilfully manipulated the space of a central hall against associated recesses, but they also took into account the criticism that it was impractical to group all family activities together. The text discussed the boundaries between sociability and privacy: 'The essential principle insisted on is that the smaller kind of house, instead of being subdivided to the greatest possible extent into tiny compartments, should at least contain one good-sized room, which, by devices such as sliding doors, can be made on occasion still larger.' Baillie Scott worked through many permutations of the open plan – and in the process made a distinctive, lasting contribution to the development of modern house planning.

Many of the defects of mass housing deplored by Baillie Scott derived from their lack of individual character or responsiveness to a particular environment. His own houses and gardens grew from their locality and terrain, and drew on local building techniques and materials. All had a distinctive character, for Baillie Scott believed that every house, no matter how small, was to be valued as a home.

Baillie Scott concluded the first chapter of the book with a rallying-cry: 'Let it be vital, local and modern; the new thought of a new age wrought with eagerness and care instead of the trite and stale copyism of forms of the past.' By matching these powerful words to the houses he built, we can see how he forged a progressive new direction in design.

CLIENTS

Many of Baillie Scott's commissions came from people who knew his designs from *Houses and Gardens* or from architectural magazines. As an established architect, he worked all over the country. In Cambridge alone, he built twelve houses, mostly for members of the University: the End House in Lady Margaret Road, for example, was commissioned by Professor J.F. Cameron, a mathematician and Master of Caius College. Whilst these academic clients admired and understood his ideas, they were not necessarily rich: Gyrt-Howe was built in 1913 to a budget of £800 for another university man, a professor of Ancient History.

The design of the smaller artistic house was not a particularly lucrative path to pursue, but Baillie Scott had private means and was not totally dependent on his practice to support his family. He was able to take a more relaxed view of his fee income than his contemporary Lutyens, who felt himself to be under constant financial constraints, and refused to consider clients with less than £20,000 to spend.

In addition to private commissions for individual homes, Baillie Scott was also involved in the experimental housing developments generated by the Garden City movement.

ABOVE: The End House, Lady Margaret Road, Cambridge, under construction c.1906, and contemporary photo of the client's son collecting butterflies in the garden.

RATIONAL PLANNING

The 'average modern house' deplored by Baillie Scott was modelled as a 'mansion in miniature' in terms of both the arrangement and the use of its space. Its occupants emulated the perceived lifestyles of the rich: the best rooms were reserved to impress guests, whilst the family was 'confined in some plastered rectangular cell' … already overcrowded with unnecessary and pretentious furniture'. Reform depended on a change of heart: the householder had to abandon all desire to 'emulate his neighbours in the matter of furnishings and the methods of life', and instead demand 'that kind of beauty which is inherent in the structure, which depends largely on proportion and does not require furniture for effect'. Such unpretentious simplicity was the foundation of Arts and Crafts house design.

The central idea of *Houses and Gardens* was that modern houses could be wonderfully spacious if their organisation were planned on more rational principles: 'There is an urgent need for reform in the plan of the average modern house, and apart from artistic considerations, it is at least desirable that it should be rationally designed.' His focus was primarily on the 'houses for the average family where space is necessarily limited and precious and it should be made the most of'. Rational planning meant that this precious space was not allocated according to precedent, but in response to patterns of use. Baillie Scott rejected the standard Victorian hierarchy of rectangular cells joined by wasted corridors, and liberated the entire volume. He established a generous hall as the place where the whole family could come together: those places used only occasionally by individuals were accommodated in aedicules which could be closed off when required.

THE HALL-HOUSE

The revival of the idea of the hall-house had wonderfully Morrisian overtones of the house-place of the medieval manor, 'where the house itself was the hall and served for every function of domestic life.' Large halls were common throughout the nineteenth century, but they tended to serve primarily as circulation spaces and stairs. Baillie Scott's hall represented a revival with a difference. It was 'a general gathering-place with its large fireplace and ample floor space: no longer a passage … [but] a necessary focus to the plan of the house'.

Baillie Scott illustrated several possibilities for the form that this hall or house-place might take. The earliest proposals were for double-height spaces: the fireplace would be tucked under a gallery which tied the upper floors in with the hall. Later designs showed an open-raftered barn-like space with lower alcoves around the edges. A highly practical development was the opening of the lower hall into adjoining spaces through large double doors. In all, the hall was the central focus of the plan. The alcoves or recesses clustered around it accommodated a range of activities: dining, seating, study. Baillie Scott imagined its habitation. He evoked the scene at night when the curtains to the dining recess were drawn, 'displaying the table bright with dainty glass and flowers, lighted by a central lamp or candles against the dark background of the seats'. For larger celebrations the table could be pulled out into the main space, and musicians invited to play on the gallery above. After the meal, the guests could withdraw to a 'bower' which shared the spaciousness and warmth of the hall, but had a more dainty treatment – in some houses large bay windows seem to have fulfilled this function. During the day, Baillie Scott suggested that children might be the main occupants of the hall, finding in it a spacious, light-filled room in which to do their schoolwork.

Baillie Scott illustrated a variety of forms of central hall. FROM ABOVE: Dining room, Falkewood; Hall or house-place showing dining recess, White Nights; Open-raftered hall of Heather Cottage. Illustrations from Houses and Gardens, *1906.*
OPPOSITE: Double-height hall at Home Close, Sibford Ferris, Oxfordshire, 1910.

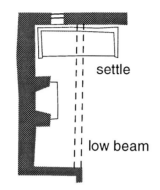

settle

low beam

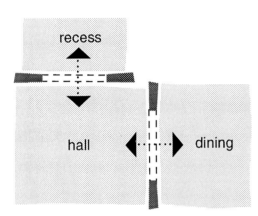

recess

hall   dining

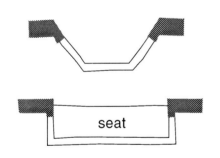

seat

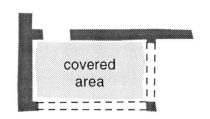

covered
area

The Elements of the Home

Several chapters of *Houses and Gardens* discussed how the various activities contained within the house could rationally be accommodated. These considerations developed into the recognisable elements of the Baillie Scott house plan during the period 1901–14. In each case they were realised and combined in different ways to relate in scale and detail to the nature of the individual house.

Fireplace Inglenook

The fireplace was seen as 'practically a substitute for the sun', drawing the family to its warmth. Its treatment reflected above all a 'breadth and simplicity' which gave it something of the scale of the open hearth of old houses. The fireplace was generally recessed in its own inglenook, carefully positioned to avoid drawing draughts across the room. The inglenook contained a simple settle and, wherever possible, a small window for light. Mindful of the need to avoid smoke, Baillie Scott often took the opportunity to make a splendid metal chimney hood.

Dining Recess

Following the model of the medieval hall-house, Baillie Scott brought dining back into the hall. However, this revival allowed for some separation, usually in the form of a recess or raised floor. Sometimes this area became a separate dining room, continuous with the hall, but closed off when required by large double doors.

Drawing Room

The extent to which additional spaces might be added to the plan depended on the overall size of the house. The drawing room was seen as the place to receive visitors, but as such it could be an element of the hall. Baillie Scott described it as a 'bower', a secluded sitting area that looked onto the hall and shared its spaciousness and warmth.

Bay Windows

The bays generated and addressed an important point in the garden. Usually south-facing, they provided an alcove for sun and light. In the earlier houses they tended to include a window seat, but later on they became a fully glazed box taking the occupant out into the garden.

Study

In Baillie Scott's time, the study usually served as the master's withdrawing room, 'for those moments when he requires privacy and solitude'. In the smaller houses, this element was taken into the hall. In houses for professional clients, the study was also a workroom, and was sometimes provided with a separate entrance.

Garden Room or Verandah

In the quest for healthy living, the beneficial effects of sunshine were much appreciated. Baillie Scott tucked a sheltered, sunny verandah under the roof of even the smallest houses. The verandahs were usually open, but sometimes glazed. In Waldbühl, a garden room was provided to alleviate the effects of the long, cold Swiss winter.

Entry Porch

Circulation was removed from the hall to avoid draughts and maintain privacy. A broad and welcoming front door generally opened into a hallway which contained a separate access for servants and a direct route to the staircase. Sometimes the hallway was paved with York stone slabs or tiles, to accentuate its role as a threshold between the external world of the street and the inner domestic environment of the main hall.

STAIRCASES

In old manor houses the staircase was often seen as an opportunity for decorative joinery work. In the same spirit of exuberance, Baillie Scott enjoyed detailing carved newel posts, turned balusters and decorated screens, some based on forms observed from old work. The stair was often set in a separate tower, which was expressed externally as a tall, gabled element. Light came from high windows above the stairs, as well as from small spyout windows angled for views on the way down. For the sake of safety, most stairs were broken into a series of short flights punctuated by landings.

KITCHEN

The kitchen was always envisaged as a separate space, although its role was fast changing. In the 1890s, even modest middle-class households expected to employ domestic help, at the very least a live-in maid. In the following decades, the established social order crumbled, and servants could no longer be taken for granted. Baillie Scott's earlier houses often included a separate back-stairs and servants' bedroom. The family domain was kept separate from the kitchen and from servants' circulation routes: judicious planning and high window sills prevented too much invasion of privacy.

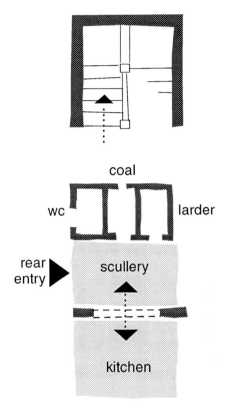

Typically, the kitchens contained both a cooking area and a separate scullery with sink, as well as a pantry, larder, coal-store and servants' wc. The early kitchens were always on the north side of the house, with a separate access from a back door. Later on, when the lady of the house had to involve herself more in the cooking, they had to become more agreeable places to work, and they were moved to the south side of the house, overlooking the garden.

OTHER OFFICES

The bathroom was usually placed directly above the kitchen, to simplify plumbing. As Baillie Scott pointed out: 'the quality of mystery has its artistic value in the house, but in the matter of plumbing it will probably only be appreciated by the plumber'. Indeed, his book contains a great deal of practical advice on matters such as the advantages of linoleum floors and draught-proof pet-doors.

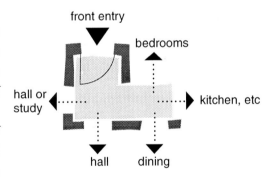

Prior to the First World War, the houses relied on fireplaces for their main source of warmth. After 1919, they tended to have central heating installations powered by coal boilers. All had electric wiring: some of the original conduits and sockets remain in position, if no longer in use. However, the levels of heat and light generated by mechanical appliances were relatively low, so the sun's penetration into the house was of prime importance.

BEDROOMS

Baillie Scott illustrated some romantic schemes for bedrooms in restful greens ornamented with flowers. Sometimes he placed the bed in a recess, so that the space could also be used during the day. In the bedroom, the fireplace served more for ventilation than warmth.

ATTICS

The steep roofs of Baillie Scott's houses usually contained attics which, being far removed from the living rooms, served a variety of uses: rumbustious playroom, detached study, or studio. In the case of some of the cheapest cottages, the bedroom was in the roof.

*48 Storey's Way, Cambridge, 1913, is a very complete
example of the ideas in* Houses and Gardens.
ABOVE: Living hall and inglenook.
OPPOSITE: Dining room seen through large double doors.

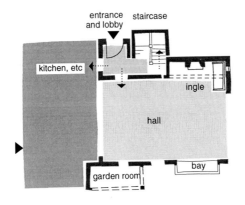

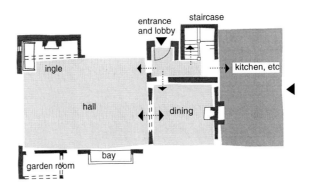

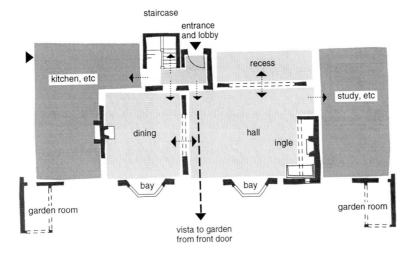

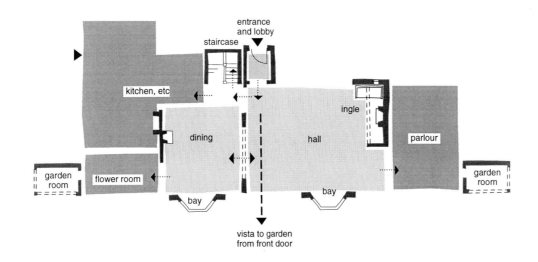

PLAN ORGANISATION

The assemblage of these generic elements to create many different house plans seemed to respond to various criteria. First, the size of the house determined the number of spaces and their rough orientation. The plans published in *Houses and Gardens* included examples of all sizes and budgets.

The hall was always the dominant element of the plan. Around it were clustered the fire inglenook, dining recess, bays, etc. The relationship of these elements was loose and varied – Baillie Scott loved to create the unexpected.

These spaces were bound together by carefully contrived axial links. Baillie Scott tended to organise internal views to focus on the fireplace, or glimpse the garden, or terminate in an alcove. Sometimes a series of doors opened to give a layered view along the length of the house. Always the most spectacular moment in a Baillie Scott house is on the view on entering, which usually connects directly through to the garden.

Many of the plans in *Houses and Gardens* were generated to illustrate a particular point, as their names suggest: 'Halcyon Cottage' (small is beautiful), 'Trevista' (three vistas), 'Crossways' (two axes intersecting), 'The Haven' (a courtyard form). The book's water-colour perspectives reinforced the message. They show spacious and empty interiors furnished only with Baillie Scott's own designs for simple furniture and rugs. Exteriors sit in flowering gardens. Set alongside the work of his contemporaries, they seem broad and simple, but spatially unique, devoid of historicist detail or fussy conceits.

After the experiments with several approaches to planning the house during the 1890s, a more consistent overall pattern began to emerge by 1905. Wherever possible, living spaces were ranged along the south front of the house. If the plot orientation allowed, they opened up to the garden through bays, garden rooms and verandahs. The north side of the house was then typically lined with the service spaces – staircase, porch, scullery and kitchen entrance, bathrooms. As the size of the house increased, further spaces were strung along the line: at Harbledown, they culminate in a parlour and pergolas to the garden, creating a long, linear house form.

FROM ABOVE: 48 Storey's Way, Cambridge, 1912–13: Oak settle in inglenook; Stair to attic.
OPPOSITE: Diagrammatic analysis of the build-up of Baillie Scott's House plans during the period 1905-14 based on: 29 Norton Way, North Letchworth, 1907; 36 Reed Pond Walk, Gidea Park, 1910; 48 Storey's Way, Cambridge, 1913; Michaels, Harbledown, 1912.

EXTERIOR

Baillie Scott's agglomerative planning tended to mean that his houses had an irregular footprint, stepping in and out around bays, stair towers and chimneys. However, he recommended, in the chapter on 'Some Forms of Plan', that 'in economic building it [was] wise to make the house itself of simple rectangular form, covered with a single space of hipped roof'. This simple roof form could be elaborated by introducing abutting wings or by building around courtyards. Most of the houses are a development of one such diagram, being essentially simple structures of load-bearing external walls carrying roofs pitched at 54.5 degrees.

Baillie Scott's second consideration was to achieve 'picturesque arrangements of roofing'. He was a master of the seemingly informal but cleverly choreographed arrangement of long roof against gable chimney and bay. 48 Storey's Way in Cambridge expresses a studied asymmetry: the long sweep of the roof which pulls down over the front door is set against the gables of the tall, thin stair tower and the kitchen wing. Any sense of imbalance is rectified by the two tall rectangular chimneys and counterweight single dormer. This felicitous arrangement contrasts with the high eaves of the south elevation and flat surface of the facade, which is broken only by two bay windows, but clad entirely in trellis.

In general Baillie Scott felt that heights should be kept as low as possible, to create the 'long snug effect which is so characteristic of the old English house'. He was most concerned when, after the war, a new Building Byelaw raised the minimum ceiling height from 7ft 6in to 8ft, and led a successful campaign to reverse the regulation.

His aim in all this was to allow the house to sit easily in its site. He was sensitive to the placing of the building to harmonise with the landscape, and particularly liked to use local materials. In the case of the suburban plot, he remarked that there it was necessary to 'make Nature harmonise with the house, or make house and Nature meet each other half-way'.

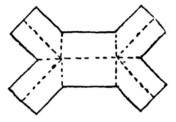

Above all, Baillie Scott was concerned to redefine 'the house which the average citizen requires, which it should be the triumph of the architect to make as perfect as circumstances permit'. His constant aim was to define a fresh option within the reach of the average householder.

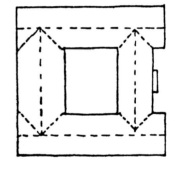

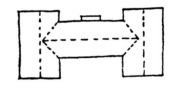

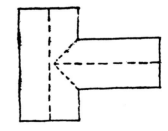

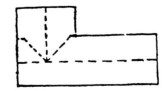

FROM ABOVE: Springcot, 1904; Heather Cottage, 1906; Roof plan diagrams.
OPPOSITE, FROM ABOVE: Garden front, 48 Storey's Way; Street elevation, 29 Norton Way North, Letchworth.

CONSTRUCTION

If the artistic house was to rely upon 'the essence of its structure' for adornment, it was imperative that this essence be understood and expressed. Baillie Scott achieved this not by structural gymnastics – his houses were always of conventional construction – but by means of materials. He sought out the essential quality of the materials, and exploited to the full the manner of their use. He wrote that plaster, for example, should have a 'characteristic surface' exaggerated by the use of sharp sand, and be finished from the trowel, not with a float. Timber was to bear the memory of its origin as a tree, and be left roughly finished from the adze when used as beams or joists. Panelling, on the other hand, had to be planed to be smooth to the touch, whilst respecting that subtle variation in grain which makes flatness hard to achieve.

This same appreciation of essential characteristics was applied to his discussion of the elements of the house. The object of windows, he stated with disarming simplicity, was 'to let light into the rooms'. But he knew that different types of glass would refract light in different ways, and that the subtle modulations of crown glass would cast fascinating shadows. Small panes would create a varied quality of light, whereas the large sheet of glass had only 'a blank and vacant stare'. As the window frame filled a hole in the wall, it had to look strong enough to support the wall above. Generally his mullioned windows were in timber with metal opening casements, and they were positioned flush with no protruding sill, allowing the surface of the wall to remain undisturbed.

Throughout *Houses and Gardens*, Baillie Scott pursued his quest to redefine the artistic house. The book ends by returning to his source of inspiration: his reverence for the old work, and his striving to recreate its spirit in 'the soul of the house'. His ultimate goal, beyond questions of cost, aspect and planning, was to achieve houses which were not shallow, showy and pretentious as most contemporary houses were, but full of a 'still, quiet earnestness which seems to lull and soothe the spirit with promises of peace'.

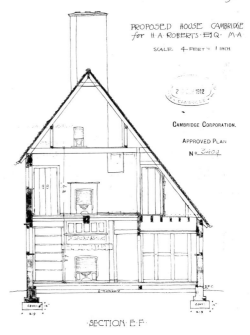

ABOVE: 48 Storey's Way, Cambridge, 1912–13: Exterior; Section from original Building Byelaws application. LEFT: Hall of Halcyon Cottage, 1906. OPPOSITE: View down main stair of 48 Storey's Way.

British Homes for Today

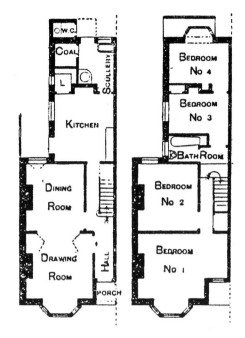

In the final chapters of *Houses and Gardens* Baillie Scott showed how his ideas of the artistic hall-house might be applied to a wide range of housing types. He felt that all houses, however small, were entitled to a sense of space and beauty. Declaring that a house had to be first of all a home, 'a roomy and comfortable setting for family life', he tried to shift the housing discussion to questions of quality rather than mere economy. Unusually for an architect of the day, Baillie Scott was interested in mass housing. From his earliest articles in *The Studio*, he railed against the terrace house, and propounded with messianic fervour an Arts and Crafts alternative initially for the average householder with artistic sensibilities. However, his real programme was broader. The proliferating terraces had destroyed traditional villages and encroached on timeless landscapes. His alternative vision of housing based on a cottage precedent eventually roused an awareness of looser, more picturesque patterns of urban development which were crystallised in the Garden City movement and realised in inter-war suburbs everywhere.

THE TERRACE HOUSE

Baillie Scott's ideas on housing reform developed in the context of the phenomenal suburban growth of the last decades of the nineteenth century. Between 1898 and 1903 an average of 150,000 houses were built each year, almost all of them in the form of the standard Victorian terrace, which comprised a front and back living room on the ground floor with a kitchen in a narrower rear extension, and two or three bedrooms on the upper floor. Over half the population of England and Wales then lived in houses of this type, many rented rather than owned by the occupants. They were built almost exclusively by firms of house-builders, largely without the assistance of architects, but making use of the increasing standardisation of building materials and the availability of catalogues for decorative details. The basic house type was adapted to allow for many variations of frontage, plot size, social nuance, regional peculiarities, elevational treatment, and decorative bombast. Fanciful names were given to individual terraces, though even this failed to lend distinction to a very repetitive environment.

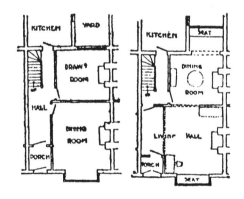

Baillie Scott suggested that all terraces should be renamed 'The Crimes'. But in Chapter 34 of *Houses and Gardens,* he showed that even these houses could be redeemed by judicious alteration, or by 'Making the Best of It'. His chief criticism of the standard terrace plan was that its subdivision into several rooms with rigidly codified uses resulted in excessively cramped spaces which became almost uninhabitable when they were stuffed with Victorian furniture. For those inescapably forced to live in such a house – and there were few alternatives – he proposed a number of modifications. His first suggestion to 'the more intelligent inhabitants of villadom' was 'to throw out the superfine and highly polished cabinets' and to replace them with furniture 'which will stand, and not be the worse for constant service'. The standard plan could then be improved by demolishing the wall between the narrow hallway and the front room, so that 'on entering the porch of such a house, we are at once in a recessed portion of the hall or house-place, with its liberal suggestion of space and freedom, instead of that chilling passage which no art of man can make homely and inviting'.

ABOVE: The standard Victorian terrace plan, and Baillie Scott's proposed modifications, which created a large living hall on the ground floor.
OPPOSITE: Leafield and Braeside, a semi-detached pair of houses on King Edward Road, Onchan, 1897.

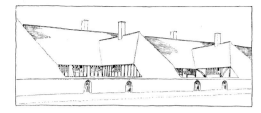

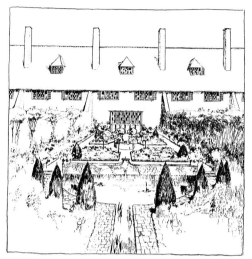

To overcome the inevitable darkness of a back room overshadowed by the kitchen extension, he suggested making an opening in the wall between the front and back rooms. 'When the whole area of the two rooms is treated as one apartment with a good fire in the front room, the dining room becomes a sort of recess in the hall and shares in its heat as well as its light, and the whole interior forms a roomy and comfortable setting for family life.' It is precisely these alterations which make many Victorian terraced houses still habitable today, a century later.

In the next chapter of *Houses and Gardens* Baillie Scott went on to propose an interesting alternative to the standard terrace house plan. Working within a 25ft-frontage, he illustrated two proposals – one for a south-facing aspect, one for the north. The questions of aspect and outlook were ignored by unvarying terrace plans. Baillie Scott was concerned to allow sun into the living rooms and to open up views of the garden that were usually blocked by the rear extension. 'The conception of the house, which primarily consists of one good-sized living room or hall, makes the position and outlook of this room a fundamental question.'

The plans are quintessential Baillie Scott. A bright, bay-windowed living room stretches across the south side of the house, connecting directly with the garden. The generous scale of this space is set against the more intimate dining recess and 'bower'. The whole plot is planned to provide vistas into the garden from within the house, and enjoyable spaces outside. An elaborate water garden leads to a grand pergola across the end of the garden. On the street side the organisation is much tighter: the kitchen accommodation comes right up to the road, forming a protected entrance courtyard from which both the house and the service quarters are accessed. The sketch of the terrace viewed from the street shows massive roofs hidden behind a street wall, which is pierced only by the entrance gates. This introverted organisation contrasts markedly with the 'smirking pretentiousness' that Baillie Scott so disliked in the self-advertising street frontage of the average terrace house.

Baillie Scott's scheme for an alternative form of terrace house was published in Houses and Gardens *in 1906. FROM ABOVE: View of terrace from the street; View from south-facing garden. RIGHT: Plan of terrace house.*

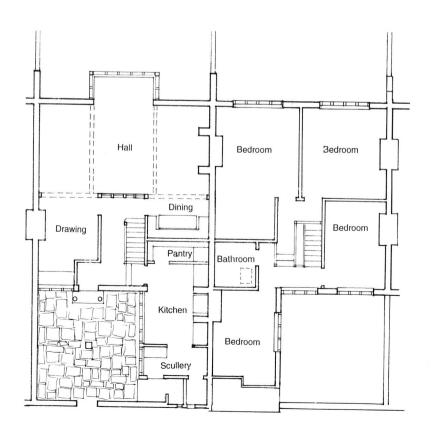

FALCON CLIFF TERRACE, 1897–8

Earlier in his career Baillie Scott built a terrace of five houses at Falcon Cliff Terrace in Douglas, Isle of Man, in which he explored a different way of applying the hall-house principle. The design dates from 1897–8 and relates closely to the centralised plans of his houses of this period, such as the 'Small Country House' published in *The Studio* in December 1897. The living rooms are clustered around a central inner hall with an inglenook fireplace and settle. This hall is lit from a tall window on the staircase half-landing. Each house has a paved back courtyard, sheltered by outhouses, onto which the living room opens through double doors.

The terrace was built by W. MacAdam, a developer on the island, and is altogether of simpler construction than Baillie Scott's grander houses of the time. The uniform rough-cast elevations are broken only by simple casement windows and cantilevered porches, in contrast with the ornate gables and decorative details applied to conventional speculatively built terraces. In their simplicity, they prefigure early modern housing schemes.

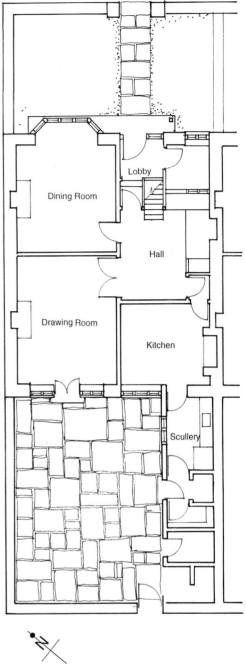

Falcon Cliff Terrace, Douglas, 1897–8.
ABOVE: Ground-floor plan.
LEFT: View from street of end-of-terrace house.

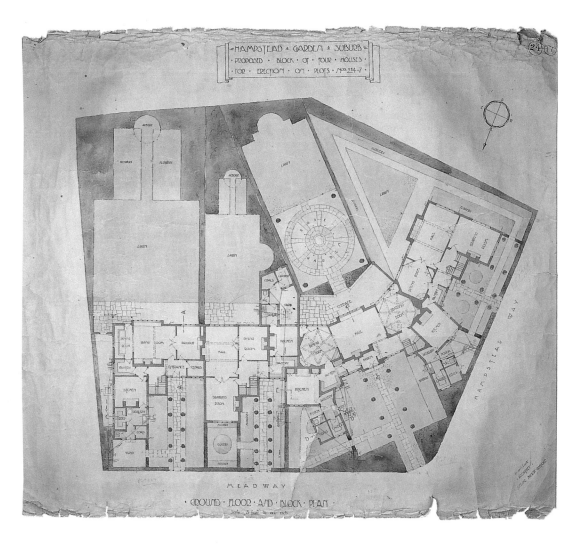

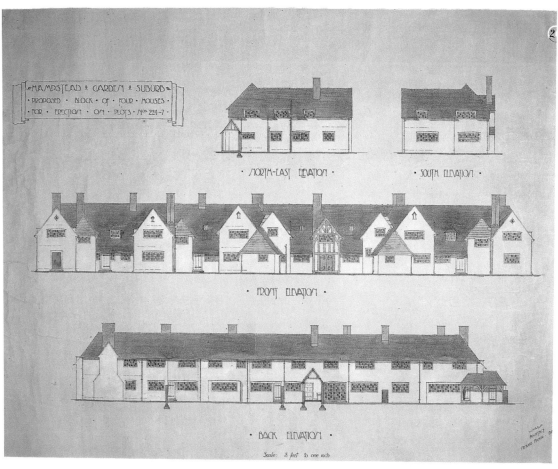

Baillie Scott's rendered drawings of the houses on Meadway, Hampstead Garden Suburb, 1907. FROM ABOVE: Ground-floor plans and site layout; Elevations.

MEADWAY, 1907

A further development of the terrace house plan is found in Baillie Scott's designs for four terraces to occupy the corner of Meadway in Hampstead Garden City Suburb. Although four plans were developed, one for each corner, only one south-facing terrace was built. The living spaces occupy the full width of the plan on the south side facing the garden, whilst the kitchen wings project back towards the street, forming compact entry court-yards within a generous plot frontage. The main living spaces are organised in sequence: the living hall is in the centre, with a dining recess at one end and double doors opening into the parlour at the other. On the opposite corner, with its different orientation, Baillie Scott proposed to distribute the living rooms along the road elevation to maintain their south-facing aspect.

Poor internal planning was not the only fault Baillie Scott found with conventional terraces. He also criticised their endless repetition of identical units regardless of location or individual ownership, 'so that an absent-minded occupant of one of them might be excused in entering his neighbour's house in mistake for his own, and would find little in its interior arrangements to undeceive him'. As the terrace steps around the corner of Meadway, the street frontage of kitchen blocks and stair towers presents a picturesque series of gable ends viewed against the long roof of the main block. Each house presents a different courtyard elevation to the street, whilst all work together as a whole. On the garden side, the swing of the roof is uninterrupted. Individual plots are subdivided by projecting 'garden rooms' and hedges, although the back gardens were never laid out as shown on the original drawing. This design takes Baillie Scott's planning concepts into a far more sophisticated organisation of form and elevation than he had hitherto achieved.

FROM ABOVE: Entrance courtyard to Meadway terrace; Views through living room to the parlour fireplace, and, looking the opposite direction, to the dining recess beyond. LEFT: Bird's-eye view and elevation of group of houses for plot 400, Hampstead Garden Suburb. This unrealised scheme illustrates the forms and grouping which Baillie Scott was developing.

PARKER AND UNWIN: THE GARDEN CITY IDEA

The application of Arts and Crafts ideals to smaller houses and housing was a concern Baillie Scott shared most closely with Raymond Unwin (1863–1940) and Barry Parker (1867–1946). Whilst Parker and Unwin's extensive work in the Garden City movement made them enormously influential, many of their ideas and images undoubtedly originated with Baillie Scott, even though he designed only a few housing schemes. Baillie Scott had the head start in the early years: he set up in practice in 1892 and from 1895 was publishing his ideas in *The Studio*; Parker and Unwin did not establish their independent practice until 1896. Parker's early sketches of double-height hall spaces with low inglenooks, bays and recesses resemble Baillie Scott's published illustrations so clearly that the likeness can be no coincidence, and Parker and Unwin's book, *The Art of Building at Home*, published in 1901, echoes many of the sentiments which Baillie Scott had set out in his earlier articles.

But although the architects shared so many ideals, and for a time lived fairly near each other, they were never close friends. They began badly in 1901 with a public disagreement over an article about Parker and Unwin in the *Daily Mail*. Baillie Scott felt the piece to be self-servingly commercial and said as much in a letter to the *Builder's Journal*. He may have recognised that the published design for a so-called '£10,000 house' was in fact Parker and Unwin's initial design for Blackwell – a commission which he eventually won. He may also have believed that Parker had copied his own designs too closely, and felt defensive of the greater delicacy and delight of his own work compared with Parker's rather solid and upright houses.

Parker and Unwin, as planners of Letchworth (1904–14) and Hampstead Garden Suburb (1905–14), were the pre-eminent proponents of the Garden City movement. Their signatures of approval are found on the top of Baillie Scott's drawings for projects in both places: a reminder that they were responsible for the day-to-day supervision of construction standards for individual projects as well as for the development of the overall planning concepts of the city plan. The Garden City housing layouts were in many ways the answer to the ubiquitous terrace development of suburbs: they incorporated employment, shopping and civic facilities and open space within the city structure. Unwin's seminal paper, 'Nothing Gained by Overcrowding' (1912), set out an analysis of the relationships between plot size, width of frontage, road development and land costs, which established a rational basis for the lower density housing developments that characterised Garden City housing.

Baillie Scott made several contributions to the design of cottages in the new garden suburbs, mainly through participation in housing competitions. In 1905 he took part in the 'Cheap Cottage Exhibition' at Letchworth. The budget for the entries was £150 per cottage, and as Baillie Scott's semi-detached pair (Elmwood Cottages) cost just over £400, they were disqualified from the prizes. However, they featured prominently in the catalogue of the exhibition, both for the clarity of their planning and for the strength of their interiors, which are focused around a broad kitchen fireplace and settle. Again in 1910, he designed a pair of exhibition houses for Gidea Park, a showpiece garden suburb near Romford in Essex. These are grouped together to create a long, low proportion to the street. The plans are centred around a generous living room which opens onto a dining recess and verandah: the more expensive house also includes a separate parlour. The show-houses were originally furnished by Heals and by the Deutsche Werkstätte with furniture and fabrics to Baillie Scott's designs.

FROM ABOVE: Illustrations from the 1910 Gidea Park exhibition catalogue of Baillie Scott's semi-detached houses at Reed Pond Walk: Interior view and advertisement offering the houses for sale at £500 (with parlour) or £375 (without); Terrace design from Houses and Gardens, *1906.*

Baillie Scott seems to have had a more successful working relationship with Raymond Unwin at Hampstead Garden Suburb. In 1909 they both contributed to a book, *Town Planning and Modern Architecture in the Hampstead Garden Suburb*, which was illustrated mostly with Baillie Scott's work. Baillie Scott did not think in planning terms of densities or road layouts: his influential contribution to the housing debate lay in his images of houses grouped together to form ordered courtyards or step around a corner. For a group of houses he took the same elements which he manipulated in single houses – gables, roofs and walls – and composed them into balanced juxtapositions of rough textured roofs, rendered gables and casement windows, whilst giving careful attention to the separate planning of individual units. The forms and picturesque layouts of these schemes were taken up in the cottage estates developed by the LCC Housing Division and their influence spread. Thus Baillie Scott provided much of the architectural imagery of the Garden City, if few of the schemes.

Suburban Houses

From the perspective of the late twentieth century it is hard to imagine how specific a creation is the English suburban house. When Baillie Scott was writing, the terrace house was the only mass housing option. His work presented a new alternative based on a cottage precedent in the casually informal layout of an English village.

In his post-war practice Baillie Scott continued to build individual houses but in the 1930s he also designed speculatively built houses for a firm of building contractors run by his son-in-law, Dudley Wallis. This work is exemplified by two schemes at Kippington, near Sevenoaks in Kent, and at Blackhills, near Esher in Surrey. Baillie Scott provided quarter-inch drawings of plans and elevations often without visiting the site or meeting a client. He found this way of working unsatisfactory, but in those lean years was glad for the work. The houses themselves are loosely based on vernacular precedents: the tile-hanging and timber-framing of Kentish farms and barns. Most are built on large plots, with sizeable gardens. They rarely include adventurous open plans, but tend to have a more conventional subdivided plan. Baillie Scott was able neither to detail them nor to supervise their construction, so they lack the quality of detail typical of his houses. However, during that period of financial and political uncertainty, the reassurance of 'timeless' traditions added to the attraction of these cottages. They presented a persuasive image of home which has quite outlived the atmosphere of their inception in countless suburban developments in all parts of the country. As Peter Davey comments in his *Arts and Crafts Architecture*: 'The builders did what the architects, for all their high ideals, failed to accomplish. They brought Arts and Crafts to the people. For a movement which had started with the ideals of Ruskin and Morris, the inter-war suburb was not an ignoble ending.' Rarely do the succeeding speculative houses achieve the strength of a Baillie Scott original – they do not dare to pull the roof right down low, overhang the eaves quite as far, or exploit the texture of their materials. Though pale imitations of the vision of architects such as Baillie Scott, these surburban vernacular houses reflect none the less the imagery of their Arts and Crafts origins.

ABOVE: 'Ready-made houses' in Sevenoaks, Kent, designed by Baillie Scott for construction by his son-in-law in the early 1930s.

Waterlow Court, 1909

Baillie Scott's most ambitious scheme at Hampstead Garden Suburb was Waterlow Court, a development of fifty flats for young working ladies built in 1908. Each unit had a single main living room – a small version of the living hall – with a bed alcove off it. Very small kitchens were sufficient as most meals were provided communally in the Central Dining Hall. A precedent for the layout of Waterlow Court was the scheme for Co-operative Houses in *Houses and Gardens*. As an alternative to a meagre row of small terrace houses in a cramped street, Baillie Scott proposed a courtyard of houses with shared facilities, such as communal gardens. 'In seeking for the type of plan which would be most suitable for such a group of houses, the College Court with its central hall and cloisters at once suggests itself. A covered approach to the central hall from the various houses is thus provided, and the whole arrangement is one which is admirably adapted to artistic treatment.'

The Co-operative Houses proposal no doubt helped to recommend Baillie Scott as architect for Waterlow Court, which also used a courtyard plan surrounded by three floors of accommodation. But despite the acknowledged precedent, the central courtyard is not at all collegiate in feel: the arched openings in white rendered walls are light and cheery. The courtyard has as its focus the gable of the central refectory, which is reached by the covered arcades. The exterior of the scheme has a quite different character, using dark brickwork with half-timbering on the upper floors. It seems almost fortified, an impression reinforced by the suggestion of a raised portcullis over the entrance gate. This forbidding expression is easily offest by the twinkle of inset tilework in the gables, and by the spacious shared gardens enclosing the court. And around the back, down by the shed, each flat has an allotment strip for the young ladies to grow flowers.

Many years later Baillie Scott told John Betjeman that Waterlow Court was one of his favourite schemes. It combines many of his aspirations in architecture, making a clear statement of an alternative way of living in cities – in small individual units combined into a building of breadth and scale, pervaded by planting and space. The flats themselves demonstrate his approach to internal planning, with alcoves that open up to maximise the spaciousness of the available floor area. Above all, Waterlow Court has a sense of enjoyment – of celebrating a place which is home.

Waterlow Court, Hampstead Garden Suburb, 1909.
FROM ABOVE: Contemporary photograph of working ladies relaxing in the courtyard; Interior of courtyard – each flat is accessed from the cloister.
LEFT: Baillie Scott's sketch of the interior of a flat, illustrating the principle of making a living space of maximum size with the bed housed in a recess.
OPPOSITE: Exterior from the south, showing allotment gardens.

The Artistic Garden

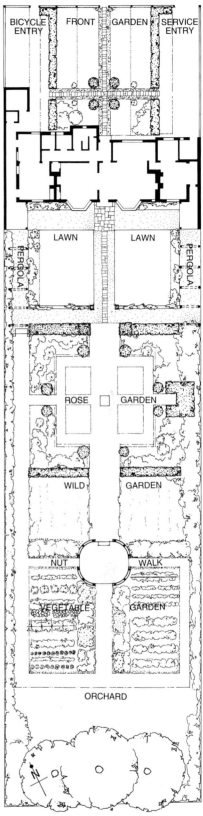

O f all the architects of the Arts and Crafts movement concerned with garden design, Baillie Scott gave most serious thought to small gardens. He designed everyday gardens, in contrast to Lutyens, Weir, Schultz, Newton, or Lorimer. And he had a more realistic feel for what was required in terms of maintenance than, for example, Gertrude Jekyll, whose own idea of a small garden was Millmead in Bramley, Surrey (77ft wide by 400ft long). Millmead is described in the first chapter of Jekyll's *Gardens for Small Country Houses* (1912): it has terraces and layers of planted dry walls, lawns and elaborate flower beds, all requiring a great deal of expertise and expenditure to maintain. Baillie Scott knew that such a garden was out of the reach of the hard-pressed suburban householder faced with a bare new building plot.

The true inventiveness of Baillie Scott's garden designs rests not so much in their elements, which were to be found in many Arts and Crafts works of the period, but in their intimate scale and their unity with the house. Baillie Scott was well aware of the contemporary debate on the relative merits of formal and natural gardens. Indeed, as he noted in the introduction to *Houses and Gardens*, books on gardens far outnumbered those on house design: 'the house as an appendage to the garden meets with a certain degree of attention; but the problems involved in house-building, furnishing and decoration have hardly been treated with the consideration they seem to deserve'.

Garden design fitted naturally into the concerns of the Arts and Crafts movement, and Baillie Scott must have been aware of the influential work of J. D. Sedding (1838–1891), and in particular his book, *Garden-Craft Old and New* (1891). Baillie Scott's own early schemes focused on the design of the houses, but around 1901–02 he seemed suddenly to realise the potential link between internal and responding external spaces. Perhaps his interest was spurred by E.S. Prior's series of three articles on 'Garden-Making' in *The Studio* from October to November 1901. These included a plan of 'An Oblong Garden' which was modest in scale and practical in intent, with a formal layout containing fruit and vegetable gardens. In *Houses and Gardens* Baillie Scott includes several designs for gardens for just such a long, thin suburban plot, but his designs extend the house planning into a world of outdoor rooms and walks.

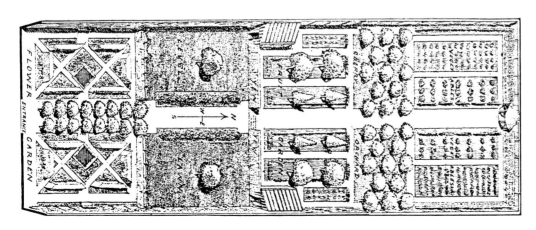

48 Storey's Way, Cambridge, 1912–13.
ABOVE: Garden plan.
LEFT: E.S. Prior's plan for 'An Oblong Garden'
The Studio, *November 1901*
OPPOSITE: View from pergola.

VISTAS

The first example of an interconnection between house and garden in Baillie Scott's work appears to be the 'Springcot' scheme, which was published in the *Builder's Journal* in December 1903. Springcot was designed as a holiday cottage and, more graphically, as an 'illustration of certain principles in garden-making'. The cottage is almost swallowed by the garden: the garden axis runs right through the central corridor, between hall and kitchen, and then continues down a shady pergola to a seat by a bright water garden at the end of the plot. The busy little garden contains nearly all of the elements that Baillie Scott was to develop in later designs. He wrote: 'One may note first of all the importance attached to vistas – vistas arranged with definite terminal effects. One may also observe the usefulness of shade in the garden as well as light, and how embowered paths may be contrasted with the brightness of open spaces.' The site is criss-crossed by a whole series of vistas, always focused on a far goal – a dovecote, pump, summer house, well, or tree. These visual axes are also paths connecting a series of enclosed and distinct garden spaces which make up the overall plan. The enjoyment of the garden comes from the sequential experience of the different elements: 'In passing through these enclosed ways, one loses all conception of the garden scheme till, at the intersection of a path, one suddenly perceives through vistas of roses and orchard trees some distant garden ornament, or perhaps a seat or a summer house; and so one becomes conscious of a scheme arranged and of well-considered effects. As in a dramatic entertainment, apartments of the garden full of tragic shade are followed by open spaces where flowers laugh in the sun.'

Houses and Gardens contained another imaginary scheme, 'Trevista', which explored further a unified planning approach: 'This is not a case of first designing a house and then laying out its immediate surrounds as a garden bearing a certain relation to it, for house and garden are here the product of a single initial idea which comprehends the whole.' From his earliest projects, Baillie Scott had demonstrated a strong spatial imagination, always sketching the internal spaces he described. In Trevista, this ability was extended to the design of the external spaces, which were linked back into the plan of the building. A central axis ran from the front gate through an entry court to a shady passage and then continued down the centre of the 100ft-wide rectangular plot: this main axis was flanked by two side paths which ran under pergolas to the pavilions at the far end of the plot. The views from the living room windows also found responses in garden features.

The ideas of the Trevista plan are closely echoed in the design for 48 Storey's Way, Cambridge (1912–13). Here both house and garden survive in good condition, and we can experience something of the intended enjoyment of the scheme. The shape of the suburban building plot is rectangular, as at Trevista: it has a 75ft-frontage and is 300ft long, with a *de facto* building line some 45ft back from the road. The plot is ordered by three axes which run the length of the site, starting from three gates in the white paling fence to the road. The central axis enters a court defined by privet hedges and lined with roses, peonies and lavender. 'On opening the front door one enters a wide and low passage, and beyond its cool shade one sees the garden room, and beyond that, one catches a glimpse of a garden vista' – Baillie Scott's description of Trevista fits this place exactly.

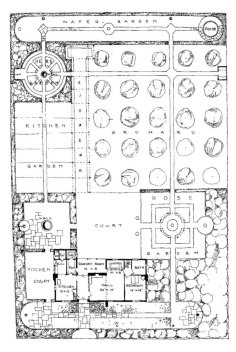

The axes establish a series of six garden spaces which are separated by yew hedges: a garden room edged by pergolas, a more formal rose garden, a contrasting slice of wild garden in which the long grass is studded with bulbs and wild flowers, a circular vinery, a kitchen garden, and, finally, a grassy orchard. This formal framework gives 'scope enough within its boundaries to create a little paradise of flowers'. The house itself extends the full width of the site, and its living rooms are oriented south, towards the garden. Indeed, when one sits in a bay window and looks back on the trellised external wall clad with still-thriving Edwardian roses, it is easy to imagine that one is already in the garden.

FROM ABOVE: View of 48 Storey's Way through the series of garden rooms; Entrance Pergola to Undershaw, Guildford, 1908 as illustrated in The Studio; *Design for Springcot garden and house, 1903 – view of house from kitchen garden and garden layout.*
OPPOSITE: Vista up the Yew Walk towards Snowshill Manor, 1926.

A Paradise of Flowers

Many years after visiting Baillie Scott at his home, John Betjeman recalled that he seemed to be surrounded by flowers. Baillie Scott had an intense love of flowers: his plant patterns were never distorted like Mackintosh's, or simplified like Voysey's, but were drawn from close observation, so they communicated their natural beauty. An assistant in his office remembered being sent to pick hawthorn blossom to study for the decorations at Waldbühl.

When it came to planting gardens, Baillie Scott had not only sound practical knowledge but strong aesthetic preferences. He hated Victorian bedding-out schemes which consisted of gaudy plants set at regular intervals, and recommended instead that Gertrude Jekyll's books be taken as 'an infallible guide'. His watercolours show a profusion of cottage garden flowers: generous clumps of delphiniums, hollyhocks, day-lilies, daisies, campanulas, lavender, pinks and asters, as well as roses climbing over trellises and pergolas. He suggested that planting should be composed as an artist chooses colours, with flowers massed together, not graduated by size. These ideas could easily be realised in small suburban gardens: 'Actual size has little to do with the effect of such a garden, and a variety of effects may be achieved in a comparatively small area by careful planning.'

ABOVE: Hawthorn pattern tiles from the master bedroom at Waldbühl, Uzwil, 1907–11.
LEFT: Inlay from a Baillie Scott cabinet in a private collection.
OPPOSITE, ABOVE: Miss Daw's 'Cottage Garden', Little Barrington, Oxfordshire. Photo by Edwin Smith. 'Many old cottage gardens, which are to be seen in our villages, show the possibilities of homely beauty which belong to such a union of use and beauty in the garden, and such a garden, worked in the spare time of its owner with a rough and ready love which is his traditional inheritance, will be profitable as well as pleasant.' (Baillie Scott, Houses and Gardens)
OPPOSITE, BELOW L. TO R.: Inlaid panel of marguerites from the secrétaire in the drawing room at Blackwell; Inlay flower panel from Manx piano in the collection of the Victoria & Albert Museum.

PRACTICALITIES

Perhaps as a consequence of his initial training at the Royal Agricultural College at Cirencester, Baillie Scott had a far more practical approach to gardens than either Gertrude Jekyll (with whom he collaborated on two schemes) or his architect contemporaries. He clearly knew the labour involved in establishing and maintaining elaborate garden schemes: 'A garden is expensive to maintain chiefly in proportion to its artificiality and in the extent to which it includes mown lawns, bedded-out flowers, and clipped hedges. It may be wiser in many cases to aim at that kind of beauty in a garden which can be achieved by assisting and directing Nature, rather than by striving to mould her to an artificial ideal.' His advice to busy householders was to opt for a wild garden – a woodland copse carpeted with wild flowers – or a grassy orchard filled with fruit blossom.

From his observations of cottage gardens, Baillie Scott determined that it was unnecessary to distinguish between pleasure gardens and kitchen gardens: such a distinction implied that there was 'no pleasure to be derived from the contemplation of plants or trees which are otherwise useful'. On the contrary, he suggested, there was every possibility of uniting use and beauty: 'In the kitchen garden one finds so many plants that have lost caste, as it were, by daring to be useful, and the scarlet runner would be as much admired as the scarlet geranium, were it not for the uses of its slender pods. The grey-green foliage and great thistle heads of the artichoke, the mimic forest of the asparagus bed, and the quaint inflorescence of the onion have a beauty of their own.' In his real understanding of the productive economy of the practical garden and his sympathy for the local landscape, he was ahead of the merely aesthetic gardeners of his time. His vision was in tune with nature – anticipating the environmental concerns of the late twentieth century – and opposed to the imposition of an increasingly urban culture.

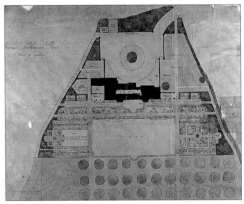

In the same way that Baillie Scott's buildings made use of local materials and methods, his gardens responded to the variations and constraints of the natural landscape. He allowed for a natural approach: 'There seems nothing quite so good as a setting for the house as a dark moorland covered with the purple of the heather. Add to this the background of a deep pine-wood and a few silver birches, and all the setting a house of grey stone will require will be a terrace enclosed with a rough wall of lichen stone.' The watercolours for Heather Cottage at Sunningdale, Berkshire, illustrate such a location. This particular scheme is given added drama by the contrast of the natural landscape with the formality of a tamed and enclosed garden.

Through all of Baillie Scott's writings runs the sense that gardens are sanctuaries from the world outside – be it wild heather moors or the relentless pace and ugliness of the industrial city. This ideal of seclusion is best expressed by the lines from a Celtic fairy tale carved over the fireplace at Green Place, a holiday house built high in the Hampshire downs for a couple from Liverpool: 'And it came to pass, upon a day of days, that they were in a green place, and they were in the sun and out of the wind, and they were near their friends and far from foes, and they could see everyone and no one could see them.'

Michaels, Harbledown, Kent, 1912.
FROM ABOVE: Pergola opening from parlour;
Original garden layout.
OPPOSITE: View of south front and terrace.

SNOWSHILL MANOR GARDEN, 1920

Snowshill Manor is the only surviving example of a Baillie Scott garden commissioned independently of a house. The client was Charles Paget Wade (1883–1956), who met Baillie Scott during the development of Hampstead Garden Suburb. Wade worked with Unwin, and made a series of wonderful line drawings to illustrate his visions of irregular urban space based on medieval towns.

Baillie Scott's planning concept for Snowshill was consistent with other works, in that it formed a series of architecturally defined garden spaces linked by a vista back to the house. But in this particular place, the enclosed courts step down into a green Cotswold valley, and are punctuated by romantic conceits designed by Wade to create 'a pleasant paradise full of sweet flowers and daintiest delights'.

Wade was a wealthy man, the heir to a West Indies sugar fortune. He purchased the sixteenth-century Snowshill Manor in 1919 to house his collection of historic craftsman-ship – an extraordinary assembly of farm carts, navigational devices from sailing ships, Samurai armour, silk-weaving looms, huge locks, and many other objects which formed a record of traditional crafts that were being lost with the advance of the machine. Wade felt deeply the loss of skills that had developed over generations since medieval times. Similarly, Baillie Scott mourned the demise of the old ways of building. Through their collaboration in this small garden, they created a haven which intensifies the sense of a particular place and its local materials, convincing us of its timeless relevance. As the garden was intended to be a statement addressed to society, it is appropriate that it is now open to the public as the property of the National Trust.

Wade appreciated the importance of architectural structure in garden design, as his description of the work shows: 'the design was planned as a series of separate courts, sunny ones contrasting with shady ones and different courts for varying moods. The plan of the garden is much more important than the flowers in it. Walls, steps and alleyways give a permanent setting. Mystery is most valuable in design; never show all there is at once, plan for enticing vistas with a hint of something "beyond".' Here we find all the characteristics of the Arts and Crafts garden, relating to a marvellously sympathetic landscape and location.

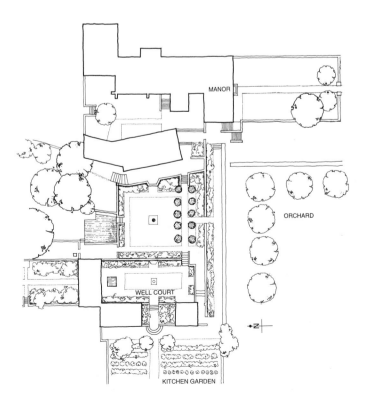

The gardens at Snowshill Manor were laid out by Baillie Scott, although the dovecote and sundials were designed by Charles Paget Wade.
FROM ABOVE: Vista along old barn past dovecot to Armillary Court; Pool.
LEFT: Plan of garden.
OPPOSITE: View of Armillary Court with Gloucestershire landscape beyond.

J.B. Priestley visited Snowshill on his English Journey in 1933, when the eccentric Wade was still in residence. He described venturing into 'one of these enchanted little valleys, these misty cups of verdure and grey ways. In this valley was a hamlet, an old church and the manor house, all of them clustered in a lovely muddle of ancient tiled roof. The house itself had a Gothic craziness. There was no sense, though an infinite antique charm, in its assembled oddity of roofs, gables, windows and doorways. There was a tiny courtyard between the house proper and a large outhouse, which had on its wall a painted wooden knight whose head was waiting to strike a big bell. Beyond the outhouse were descending squares of garden, where a stream wandered from one clear carp pond to another, slipping past clumps of miniature box, marjoram, rue and thyme, and the shadow of yews. Olivia and Malvolio would have been at home anywhere in this garden.' Priestley's account still rings true.

The Art of Building

From around 1900 Baillie Scott was increasingly occupied with developing methods of using ordinary materials to draw poetry out of the very fabric of the building. He moved away from the elaborate pattern-making and artistry of his earlier houses (although he was still willing to revive them on demand, as Waldbühl shows), and modelled his work on the plain interiors of old manor houses. His buildings relied for effect 'on the very essence of their structure', but this structure had to be made eloquent.

Baillie Scott wrote that 'the art of building was being undermined from two directions. On the one hand, the 'mechanical ideal' of regularity and smoothness was devaluing the craftsman's role of giving 'a finished education to those materials which possess the necessary qualities for development, and letting poorer materials depend on the suggestion of their natural graces'. On the other, the architect's concern with style was diverting his attention from practical building, so that 'architecture becomes a kind of dilettante precious cult, practised by eminent gentlemen, who play an elaborate game with classic columns or Gothic pinnacles, as the case may be'. The solution, in his view, was to become aware of the nature of materials and realise their full possibilities. The art of building was an 'art … concerned with the arrangement of simple things, in simple and direct ways. We have to depolarise our minds and look at things as they really are.'

The first step was to consider the materials of building, and uncover the variations inherent in the seams of stone, the clay of bricks, or the pattern of wood. Having become aware of the nature of the materials, one could then begin to learn how to use them – drawing not only on traditional methods, but on 'a new world of art' which Baillie Scott described as 'a kind of rude natural mosaic [which] if rightly done implies the use of materials in the right way, in as much as it develops to the utmost their possibilities, instead of obliterating their character by forcing them into preconceived academic formulas.'

Baillie Scott's own experiments with the treatment of materials are manifested in the rich palette of textures in his houses. A contemporary described this in the *Architects' Journal* in 1925: 'His plain brick wall is a joy. There is the same difference between it and the average brick wall that there is between a Persian rug and an Axminster carpet.' Texture, however, was not seen as a goal in itself, but as the result of a process: 'There is no special merit in making any surface rough or smooth. Texture is mainly valuable in so far as it expresses the inherent character of the particular material.'

'Character' was the ideal that Baillie Scott advocated over mechanical perfection, which he felt to be unattainable in building. In a 1909 lecture called 'Ideals in Building, False and True', he declared 'we find everywhere slight deviations from regularity; as with outlines so with surfaces, each has its proper characteristic texture. Such slight modifications, each in itself perhaps hardly perceptible, will have an effect and in the end produce that slight difference which makes all the difference.' Baillie Scott's own working drawings seem to have been mainly unruled, and he encouraged others to 'draw as much as possible free-hand, and even with charcoal on brown paper, in order to realise the qualities of lines and surfaces'.

FROM ABOVE: Construction expressed. Beam over the inglenook fireplace at Five Gables, Cambridge, 1897–8; Framed wall with brick infill at 48 Storey's Way, Cambridge, 1912–13.
OPPOSITE: Building in local materials. Clunch in entrance courtyard at Michaels, Harbledown, Kent, 1912.

Baillie Scott called on architects to understand materials, to add to the knowledge of craftsmen. In the early years he expected his assistants to be skilled in trades and capable of demonstrating what was required on site. Whilst he himself never took up a craft, he was always keen to find highly skilled traditional workers. He relied on the plasterer Bankart, for example, to carry out many decorative commissions for him.

Although some details were repeated from house to house, Baillie Scott generally designed the elements in response to each commission. Doors, fireplaces, skirtings, architraves, window latches and hinges were usually made afresh for each house, establishing a a unique identity. Elaborate in the early years, these elements evolved to an essential simplicity in his mature work.

MATERIALS

'Every kind of material used in building has its proper texture, but this seems to be rightly expressed only when it arrives as a kind of by-product, as the outcome of a natural and unaffected use of material.' Baillie Scott looked to draw out the nature of the materials and leave the mark of their working: 'Art takes up the materials sympathetically, affectionately, and discerns some character to be developed by proper handling'. He outlined his approach to each material in an article, 'The Art of Building with Special Reference to the Use and Abuse of Building Materials', published in the *British Architect* in 1910.

STONE

'We have in many districts stones of various kinds for building; and in most of these districts we have object-lessons in old buildings, showing how the stones may be beautifully used. But our modern architects, obsessed by classical tradition and the grand manner, will take no hints from materials, and demand only smoothness and regularity, varied occasionally by dreary rustication – the masonry of the drawing board and T-square. But the art of masonry is not a matter of ruling lines on a drawing board, but a matter of arranging stones one upon another, taking advantage of every passing accident.

'A visit to the site of our building may disclose, perhaps, that flints are the essential local materials for walling. What a palette is there for the artist, of tones of pearly grey; what a variety of textures can be obtained, too. Here the soft rounded outlines of the uncut stone, and here to mark some special feature, the cut flints. The surfaces of the walling enriched, perhaps, with the shivers of the broken flints set into the joints, or notes of red brick or brown stone.

'It is a kind of natural mosaic; and if rightly done, implies the use of materials in the right way, in as much as it develops to the utmost of their possibilities, instead of obliterating their character by forcing them into preconceived academic formulas.'

BRICK

'A brick is, after all, a piece of baked clay, and its beauty consists in its character. It should have the characteristic surface and texture of another earth. It should be of the earth earthy. And so our bricks must first of all express the true inwardness of the stuff they are made of. This quality was gained in the old times by not pressing the clay too exactly into the box which formed its mould, so that its angles and arrises, instead of being straight and sharp, still retained their clayey outlines, and the surface presented those striations and fissures which are characteristic of clay. Then as to colour: a tint which is subtly varied must be more beautiful than a uniform shade, and more in harmony with natural surroundings. The mortar lines should be neither too light nor too dark in tone, but introduce into the colour scheme a tone of neutral grey – helping to give it that kind of bloom, that indescribable quality of tone, which we find in old brickwork.'

FROM ABOVE: Garden facade of Michaels, Harbledown, Kent, 1912; Rendered gables at Church Rate Corner, Cambridge, 1924 – the render was laid off in regular sweeps of the float.

RENDER

'On the exterior of a house a level cemented stone wall is dull, but if the stone wall is left with its natural facets, and then whitewashed instead of cemented, each of its planes reflects a different feature of its surroundings. One with an upward slope reflects the blue of the sky, and another sloping downwards, the green of the grass, and this gives colour and interest to the wall.'

TILES

'In the matter of roofing materials, the most important quality is texture, and so tiles must be thick; and if their new colour, as is generally the case, is too even in tint to be good, they must have such a texture as will weather and vegetate quickly. It is most important also, that the tiles should have those slight irregularities of form and surface which give such interest and charm to old roofs. Nothing is so fatal to the beauty of a roof as tiles which are absolutely regular – giving the effect of a surface ruled with absolutely rigid horizontal lines. You might just as well cover your building with galvanised iron at once. There are at present, perhaps, no entirely satisfactory tiles made from the point of view of the building artist.'

TIMBER

'In dealing with timber there are two main ideals which may be followed. In the case of timber which has no hidden beauties to bring to light by a high finish – it is wise to aim at securing some suggestion of those natural graces which belong to its living existence as a tree. In the case of other special timbers, we give up this natural beauty for those qualities that can only be educed by a high degree of finish. The great thing is not to stop between these two ideals. By the use of hand tools, at any rate for finishing the work, we cannot go far wrong. It is better to finish such a timber as oak with the adze instead of the plane. Even for such materials as mahogany, rosewood and the like. I don't want an absolute level surface or straightness of line; but just such subtle undulations as a sculptor might make in highly finished marble. The surface must just so far be alive as that. And then not glassy French polish with its disconcerting stare, that is like that excess of in glossiness and shininess in boots and hat which we associate with a certain type of City gentleman. Instead of that, let us have a quiet unobtrusive sheen which a wax polish gives.

'In woodcarving, what suggestions has the material to offer? We must respect its limitations and possibilities, and our woodcarving must be primarily just another means of educating the woodenness of the wood. That is the main characteristic which strikes us in old work. The woodwork is essentially wooden: there is a kind of blunt knobbiness about it.'

PLASTERWORK

'There are two points in regard to plasterwork which I should like to bring before you. One is texture. Do not necessarily finish your plaster with fine stuff, but preserve the texture which the sand gives, and finish from the float with subtle variations in plane. In arrises do not work to a rigid line such as is given by a cement or a wooden bead, but let the line of the arris take the characteristic line which results from deviations in plane of the surface of the plaster; and let this slight waviness of line occur in your plaster cornices as vague and soft in its outlines as waves of the sea. Let the finished plaster still retain some hint that it was soft and yielding when used: let it flow round the woodwork, perhaps engulfing it partially, as if it had risen like a flood which has been frozen. Then as to colour – the natural tint given by the sand will often be found to be a good one, and in such cases the plaster may be left untinted. If, however, the plastering is tinted, let it be for choice some tint which is germane to the material – an earthy colour, such as ochre.'

Baillie Scott generally designed the details afresh for each house.
FROM ABOVE: Door hinge, 48 Storey's Way, Cambridge, 1913; Decorative plasterwork detail of hop flowers and fruit over the fireplace at Pilgrims, Chilham, Kent, 1920 – a local reference from an area renowned for hop growing.

METALWORK

'In the treatment of wrought-iron work, the best forms will be found to be those which suggest that this cold and hard substance was once, in the heat of the furnace, soft and ductile. And so with brass, and leadiness of lead.'

GLASS

'In such a smooth material as glass, the old crown glass is much better than modern sheet glass. Used in lead or wooden frames in small panes it meets the eye with a friendly twinkle instead of a sullen glare, and the main beauty of all undulations, especially in polished surfaces, is that they give broken reflections instead of glare.

'The main difference between ancient and modern methods of building is that while the former allowed every material to be used to express its proper character, the latter has the effect of destroying character by a process of education which tends to make every surface mechanically level and smooth, and every line straight – a process varied at times by the direct aim to obtain "texture". Now, under the influence of mechanical ideals, building has become almost entirely machine-made, the old building art is lost to us, and wherever the builder touches the country he desecrates and disfigures it.'

SLATES

'Slates have the defect that they do not readily yield to nature's inimitable colouring. The rougher and thicker they are the better the artist in building will like them; and except in their own special locality, he will perhaps prefer a good grey tone to the more fashionable green. There is a kind of harshness about slates which make them specially at home in bleak and barren uplands, or in wind-swept open spaces by the sea; while the kindly warmth of tiles makes them more adapted in wooded and sheltered places.'

GLAZED TILES

'It is a difficult matter for the building artist to find a modern glazed tile which he can use. The manufacturers have all aimed at a mechanical regularity of shape, uniformity of pattern and staring glassiness of glaze, which make practically all modern tiles impossible. Certain modern makers have produced dull tiles which err on the other side, and have a dead lacklustre aspect. Only in the old Dutch tiles does the glaze have a thick and creamy quality of subtly varied tones; and in form, texture, and patterning, they are full of individual character. The drawings on these tiles would probably be a matter of scorn to any modern draughtsman, and yet they are perfect in their way, because they speak eloquently of material and process of manufacture.'

'Everywhere mechanical perfection gives way to expression of character.'
ABOVE: Repoussé copper chimney hood, White Lodge, Wantage, 1899.
OPPOSITE, FROM ABOVE: Sconce from the fireplace for Glencrutchery House, Douglas, 1897; Roses from a firebasket at Waldbühl, Uzwil, 1910.

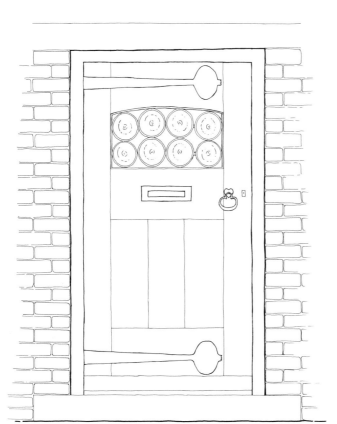

Five Gables, 1897–8.

Castletown Police Station, 1900.

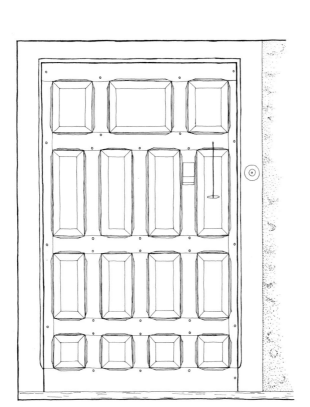

Green Place, 1906.

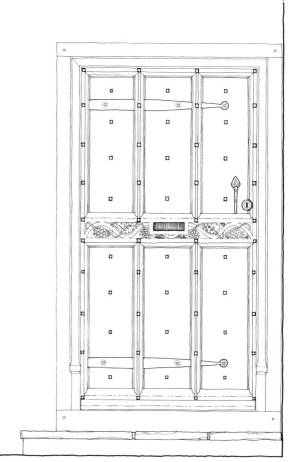

48 Storey's Way, 1912–13.

Winscombe, Crowborough, 1901.

Church Rate Corner, 1924.

Six front doors. For each house Baillie Scott invented a vocabulary of detail, encompassing doors, architraves and skirtings. There was also an internal hierarchy starting with the front door. Doors might be boarded, panelled, carved or covered with metalwork.

'The casement window will give opportunities for some
interesting blacksmith's work in the form of casement stays
and fasteners.'
The design of the door latches and hinges was also specific
to each house, commissioned wherever possible from the
local blacksmith.

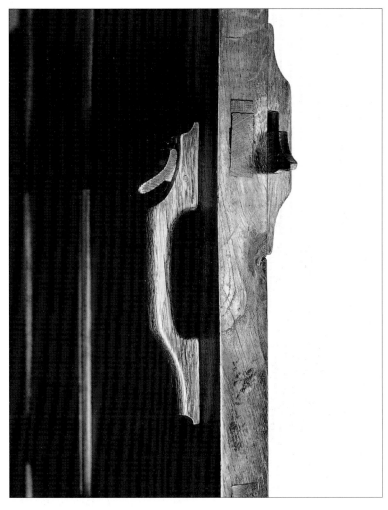

THE FIREPLACE AND ITS TREATMENT

The fireplace was for Baillie Scott the symbolic centre of the home. 'In the house the fire is practically a substitute for the sun, and it bears the same relation to the household as the sun does to the landscape. The cheerfulness we experience from the fire is akin to the delight which sunlight brings.' The fireplace had to fulfil both a symbolic and a practical role. Baillie Scott sought a 'simplicity and breadth of effect' in the design. He regarded the inglenook as an enlargement of the fireplace itself, and provided a settle which allowed the fire to be enjoyed at close quarters.

The materials of the fireplace clearly had to be incombustible – brick, stone, glazed tiles. Baillie Scott suggested that this was a point at which the structure of the house could be revealed, and stripped back the plaster to show the brick beneath. The practical requirement to avoid smoking chimneys gave him the opportunity to design decorative metal fire hood.

The fireplace was the focus for Baillie Scott's design language for the whole house. By comparing three fireplaces, we can see the evolution of his design. In his earliest articles in *The Studio* he saw the fireplace as a romantic element. In the description of 'A Small Country House' published in December 1897, the dining room inglenook is a 'most striking feature, with its red-brick back, Dutch tiles and cooper hood and its wide brick hearth'. In contrast, the fireplace in the white drawing room at Blackwell is altogether a daintier ingle, suggesting 'a charmed territory where everything shall be in harmony'. In 1924, after years of refining and stripping back his design, he made the very simplest statement with the fireplace at Church Rate Corner – a hole in the wall with massive oak mantle shelf above. Stripped of romance and rhetoric, its simplicity makes it perhaps the most eloquent.

Fireplace inglenooks compared.
ABOVE: Glazed tiling on bedroom fireplace at Five Gables, Cambridge, 1897–8.
BELOW: Fireplace in study, Church Rate Corner, Cambridge, 1924.
OPPOSITE, FROM ABOVE: Dining room at Five Gables, Cambridge, 1897–8; Fireplace in white drawing room, Blackwell, Westmorland, 1898.

Church Rate Corner, Cambridge, 1924

It has been suggested that Baillie Scott's work after the First World War is of no creative interest. Church Rate Corner shows, on the contrary, that he continued his search for simplicity and texture when supported by a progressive client. This house has a spareness far removed from the early decorated work. Each detail is carefully realised. The fireplaces are minimal, brick-edged holes in the wall crowned by solid oak mantle shelves. The bay window has a glazed framework which stretches from floor to ceiling, acting to form a screen across the opening. The architraves which form the junctions between frame and plaster are of a simple elliptical shape; the elegant bow of a door-catch adorns each panelled door. The house also contains a number of technical advances: the first-floor beams are in steel, rather than exposed oak; the external walls are of cavity construction, with a well-ventilated air gap; and there is a gravity-fed central heating system, which is still in operation, with the addition of a new gas boiler. In Baillie Scott's work, however, these innovations are supported by very traditional construction methods.

Church Rate Corner has all the intensity of the Red House built thirty years earlier – but none of its medieval imagery. Stripped of all derived references, it offered an alternative vision for architecture in the 1920s: the development of the art of building to embrace new techniques, while retaining the timeless qualities that are so inspiring in traditional buildings – the variations in light, the contrasting textures of materials, the celebration of the gardens beyond, the intimacy of a home.

Church Rate Corner, Cambridge, 1924.
ABOVE: Vista along passage to study window.
LEFT: Kitchen.
OPPOSITE: Bay window.

In Conclusion

For many of the architects of the Arts and Crafts movement, practice ended with the outbreak of the First World War. Voysey's work ceased almost entirely. Baillie Scott lay low during the war years, restoring a fifteenth-century yeoman's house in Great Chart, Kent, and enjoying the real contact with old work. After the war he set up again in practice in London with his former assistant, A. E. Beresford. Their partnership quickly flourished, but in a changed world. The architectural establishment and its clients had been seduced by Lutyens's 'High Game' and its stylistic manoeuvrings. Aided and abetted by the pragmatic Beresford, Baillie Scott designed several thin Georgian houses with builderly details but a careless disregard for symmetry. Most of the time, however, the practice continued to design in the vernacular vein – which was seen as 'Tudor' in the style-conscious 1920s. In addition to a succession of smaller projects, some very sizeable commissions were completed, such as the Gatehouse at Limpsfield, Surrey (1923), and Ashwood at Woking for Mr Derry of Derry & Thoms (1928). The workload reached new heights in the 1920s, but was vulnerable to the economic instabilities of the 1930s, and in its final years the practice was largely kept going by speculative designs for 'ready-made' houses built by Baillie Scott's son-in-law, Dudley Wallis. At the outbreak of the Second World War in 1939, when Baillie Scott was nearly seventy-years-old, both partners retired and the office archives were put into store – where they perished in the Blitz.

In his wide-ranging assessment of the Arts and Crafts, Peter Davey categorises the work of Baillie Scott as part of the movement's decline. This impression is fostered by Baillie Scott's second book, which was published in 1933. This shares the title of his first book – *Houses and Gardens* – but not its convincing propositions. It has no real message: it was simply a sales pitch when times were hard. Co-authored with Beresford, whose bantering style makes uncomfortable reading, it pushed the appeal of their traditional cottages in beautiful old England. Having been 'advanced' in the 1890s, the architects who remained faithful to Arts and Crafts ideas became by imperceptible steps 'traditional', and even, by the 1930s, 'reactionary'. They were overtaken by the brave new world of the Modern Movement.

Architects such as Baillie Scott and Voysey were extremely conscious of the differences between their work and Modernism: they hated the new movement's naive disregard for location, sound construction, and materiality. In turn, the younger generation devoted a lot of rhetoric to distancing themselves and their work from old attitudes based on tradition. 'Architecture is stifled by custom', Le Corbusier pronounced. In his recent analysis of the intellectual basis of the Modern Movement, Colin Rowe put forward a set of oppositions which polarised the two camps, '...the one set assumed [by the Modernists] to be good and the other highly dubious, to say the least. Building/form; real/ideal; public/private; dynamic/static; fact/fantasy; engineering/architecture; innovation/custom; future/past; feeling/thinking (which last pair is sometime inverted).' The Modernists went for the first in each pair, whilst Baillie Scott clearly found himself on the opposite side of the fence.

Notwithstanding the traditional/modern divide of the inter-war years, the Modern Movement can trace its origins to the Arts and Crafts in Britain. The German and Austrian 'Werkstätte' were based on the example of the English art-workers; Loos visited England

and looked at Baillie Scott houses; the 1927 Weissenhof housing revisited some of his house-planning ideas. Indeed, there has been a tendency, originating with Pevsner's *Pioneers of the Modern Movement* of 1936, to see the Arts and Crafts as nothing more than a forerunner of international Modernism – which would mean that its relevance expired with the Bauhaus. Kornwolf's monograph of 1972 adopted this point of view, devoting a great deal of effort to tracing the tenuous influence of Baillie Scott in the work of the mainstream Modernists.

From today's vantage point, it is apparent that the gulf between Baillie Scott's ideas and the continuing explorations of twentieth-century architecture was not so great. Stylistic differences should not be allowed to obscure the important issues addressed by both the Arts and Crafts and the Modern Movement: the quality of life in industrialised society, the processes of making buildings, urban development in harmony with nature. In his articles in *The Studio* from 1895 to 1914, in his strong links with the formative years of the Arts and Crafts movement in Germany and Austria, and in his architectural practice, Baillie Scott played an important role in the debate. The main themes of his agenda – the development of alternative small houses for the average householder, open and spacious planning, continuity of internal and external space, exploration of the rich textures of materials – have been of continuing importance. Far from marking the end of the Arts and Crafts movement, Baillie Scott's contribution advanced its ideals to enduring relevance.

Case Studies

The following eight projects have been selected to illustrate in greater depth the scope of Baillie Scott's work. They range in scale from a small cottage (29 Norton Way, North Letchworth) to a major manor house (Waldbühl) or large courtyard of cooperative dwellings (Waterlow Court); in concept from the elaborately decorative (Blackwell) to the simply textured (48 Storey's Way); and in time from his earliest house of 1892 (The Red House) to a late exploration of still fresh directions in 1924 (Church Rate Corner). The case studies focus on those houses which retain many of their original features and convey a good sense of the atmosphere of Baillie Scott's designs. Plans are included for each house, annotated by numbers. The key is the same for all schemes.

KEY TO PLANS			
	7 Garden Room	15 Larder	23 Bedroom
	8 Flower Room	16 Pantry	24 Bathroom
1 Hall	9 Billiard Room	17 Fuel	25 Bathroom
2 Lobby	10 Cloakroom	18 Laundry	26 Landing
3 Dining Room	11 Kitchen	19 Drying Room	27 Gallery
4 Drawing Room	12 Servery	20 Cloakroom	28 Attic
5 Study	13 Servants' Room	21 Garage	29 Servant
6 Children's Room	14 Scullery	22 Bicycles	30 Linen

The Red House

Location:	Douglas, Isle of Man
Date:	1892–3 The foundation stone reads: 'This stone was laid by Mackay Hugh Baillie Scott – aged 1 year 5 mo. – October 20 1892.'
Client:	M.H. Baillie Scott
Construction:	External walls: red brick, tile-hanging, timber frame with render panels.
Roof:	Red plain tiles.
Present condition:	Generally very good, although brickwork repointing is unfortunate, as is the painting of a chimney.
Garden:	No original layout apart from the terrace.
Records:	No original drawings.
Publication:	Never fully published. Sketch in the *Building News,* 21 April 1893. Three photographs in *Dekorative Kunst,* 1900.

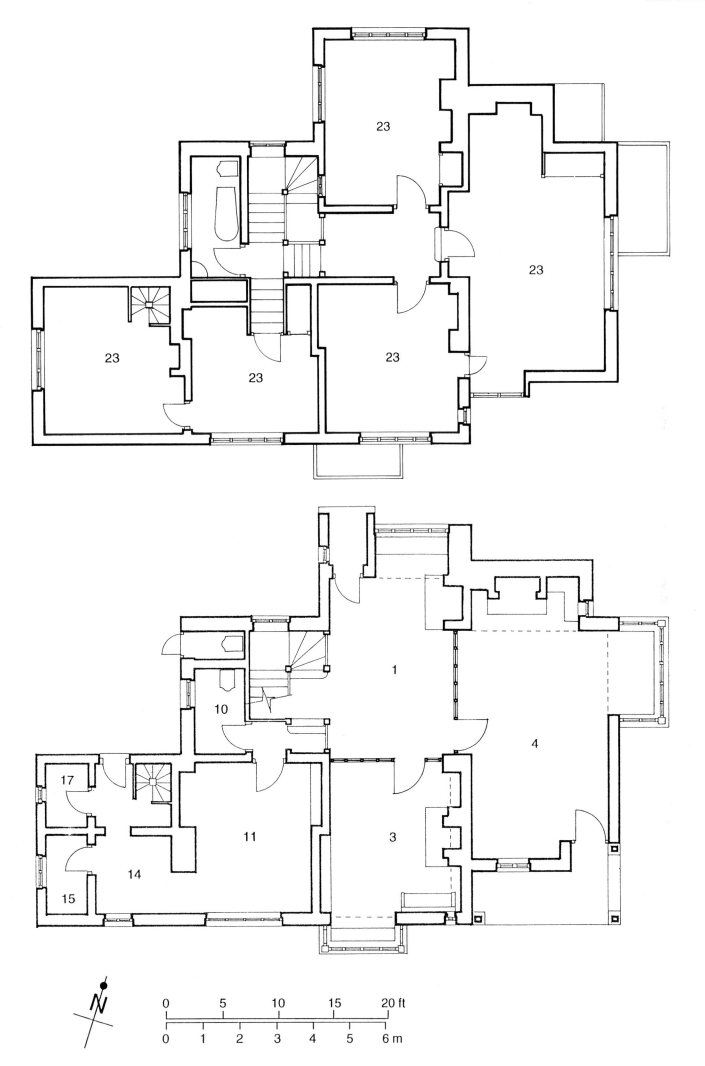

Blackwell

Location:	South of Bowness, Westmorland (now Cumbria), on Lake Windermere
Date:	1898–9
Client:	Sir Edward Holt (twice Lord Mayor of Manchester)
Construction:	External walls: roughcast render on masonry, sandstone window surrounds and mullions.
Roof:	Westmorland green slate, massive traditional Lakeland chimneys.
Present condition:	Used as a school until about 1971, presently offices – and sadly uncared for. The fabric is in poor condition and at risk of major problems.
Garden:	Evidence of some landscaping in south-facing terraces and tennis courts. Original driveway (no longer used) retains lodge and entrance gate-posts into courtyard. The huge tree seen in original photos of the entrance courtyard has now gone.
Records:	No original drawings.
Publication:	Extensively published in journals and in Baillie Scott (1906) *Houses and Gardens.*

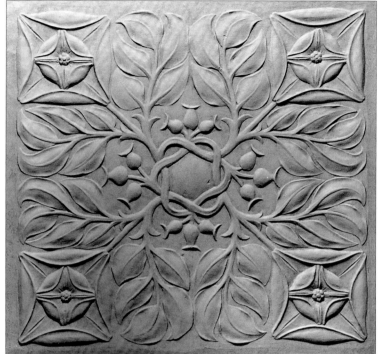

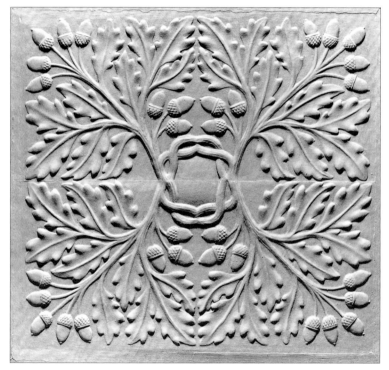

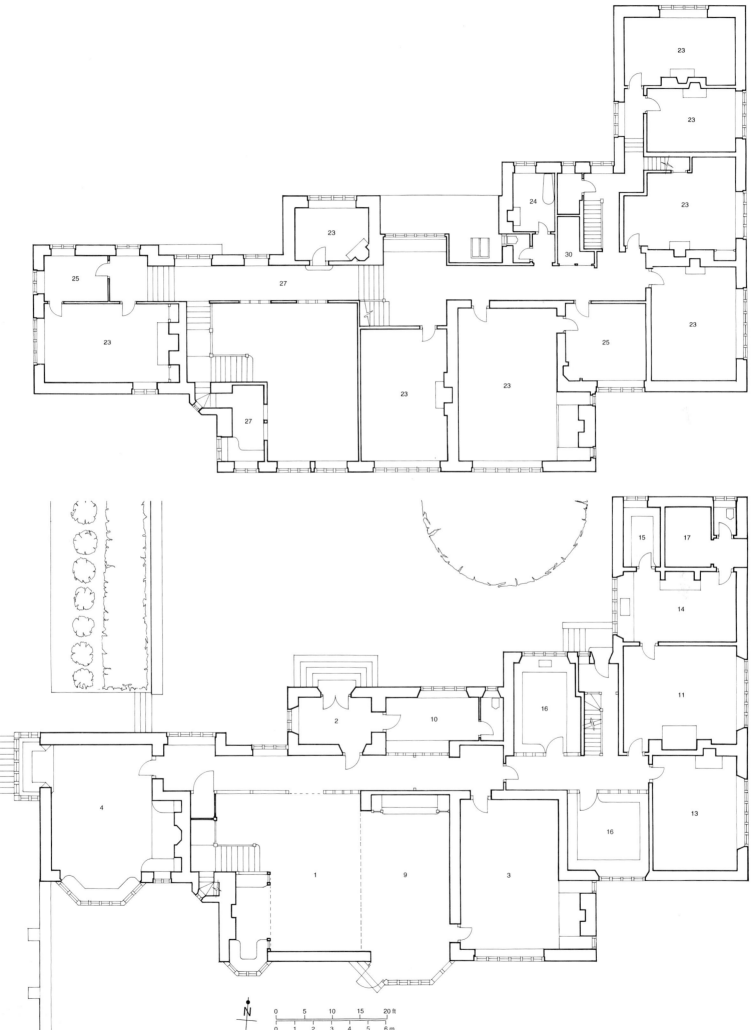

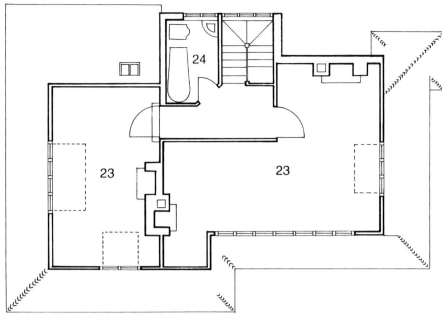

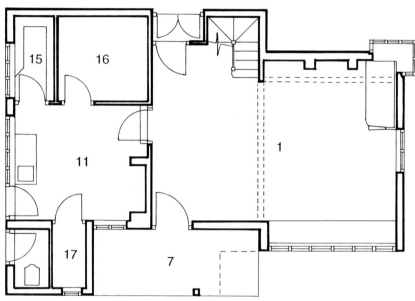

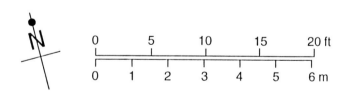

Cottage in Letchworth Garden City

Location:	29 Norton Way North, Letchworth, Hertfordshire
Date:	1907 Approval signed by Barry Parker for Plot 164.
Client:	S.W. Palmer, a local builder who built the house for himself.
Construction:	External walls: 9in brickwork with external rough-cast cement render (two parts fine gravel, one part cement).
Roof:	Bedford red clay plain tiles.
Present condition:	Good.
Garden:	Not designed by Baillie Scott.
Records:	Original drawings and application form submitted to Letchworth Garden City in Garden City Archive.
Publication:	Not published.

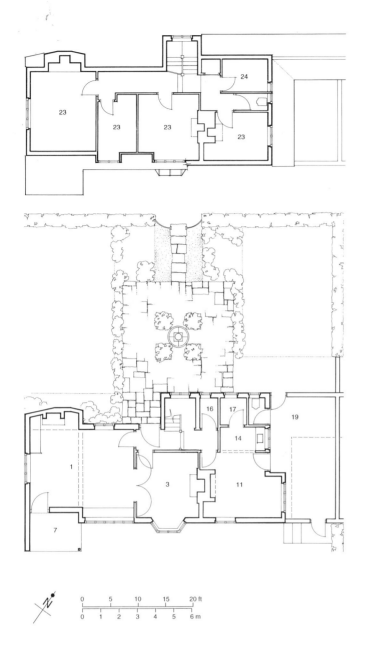

Semi-Detached Houses, Gidea Park

Location:	36 and 38 Reed Pond Walk, Gidea Park, Essex
Date:	1910–11
Client:	Gidea Park Development Co.
Construction:	External walls: 9in brickwork with external render and raised pargetting.
Roof:	Clay plain tiles.
Present condition:	Internal additions and alterations.
Garden:	One front garden has original sundial and paving.
Records:	No original drawings.
Publication:	Catalogue of the Gidea Park exhibition; contemporary periodicals.
Notes:	Built as part of a Garden Suburb exhibition; originally furnished by Heals with Baillie Scott fabrics from the Deutsche Werkstätte.

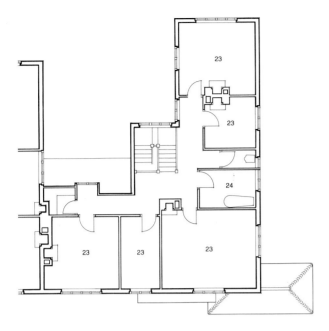

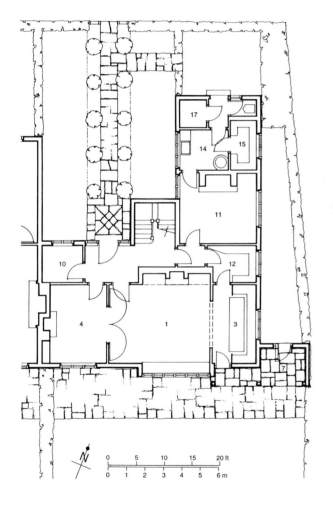

Terrace of Houses, Meadway

Location:	Corner of Meadway, Hampstead Garden Suburb
Date:	1908 Approval signed by Barry Parker.
Client:	Hampstead Garden Suburb Development Co.
Present condition:	Some additional and internal alterations, generally good.
Garden:	Layout suggested on Baillie Scott's drawing not carried out.
Records:	Original drawings in archives of Hampstead Garden Suburb Trust.
Publication:	Raymond Unwin *et al* (1909) *Town Planning in Hampstead Garden Suburb*; *The Architect*, 18 June 1909.

Waterlow Court

Location:	Heath Close, Hampstead Garden Suburb
Date:	1908–09 Approval by Hampstead Garden Suburb Trust signed by Raymond Unwin, 14 October 1908.
Client:	Associate Homes for Working Ladies for the Improved Industrial Dwelling Co. Ltd.
Construction:	External walls: 9in brickwork (Hemel Hempstead purple stocks); part timber-framing in oak with rendered panels; internal brickwork elevations rendered.
Roof:	Bedford red clay plain tiles.
Present condition:	Good, after recent programme of repairs.
Garden:	Original layout still exists, including allotment beds.
Records:	Original drawings in archives of Hampstead Garden Suburb Trust.
Publication:	Widely published: *The Builder,* 10 July 1909, 30 August 1912, and 9 May 1919; *British Architect,* 9 July 1909; *Studio Yearbook,* 1910, Baillie Scott & Beresford (1933) *Houses and Gardens.*

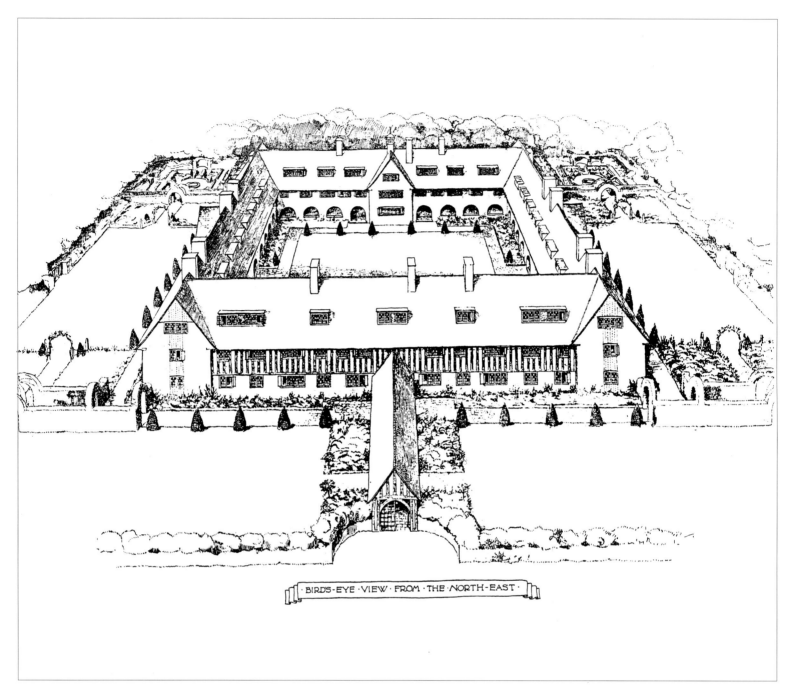

·BIRD'S·EYE·VIEW·FROM·THE·NORTH·EAST·

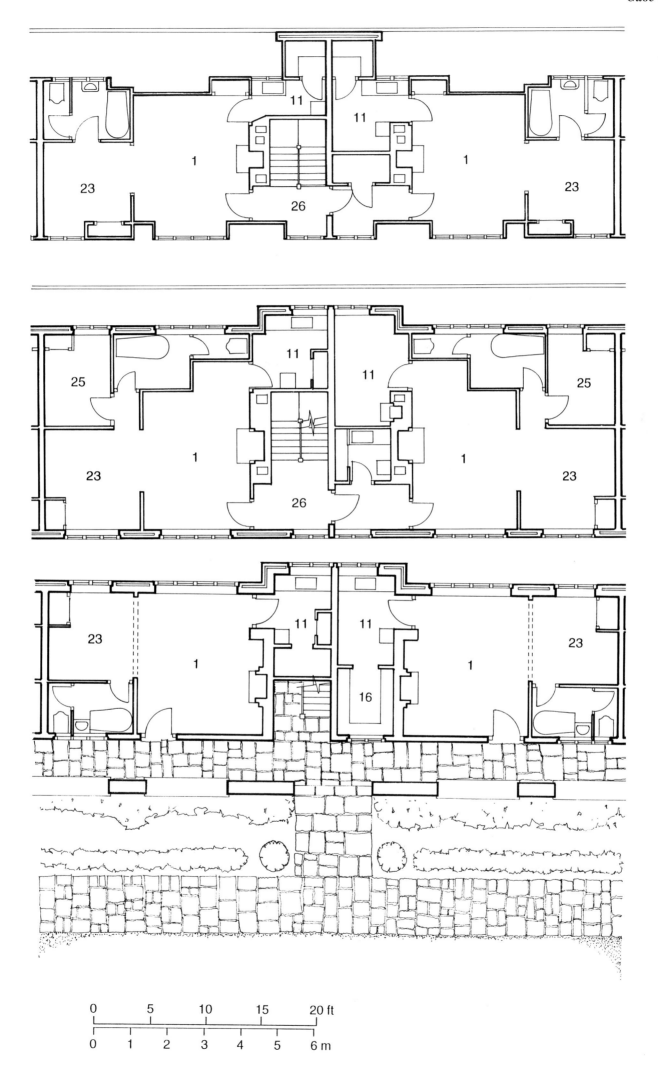

48 Storey's Way

Location:	48 Storey's Way, Cambridge
Date:	Building consent dated October 1912.
Client:	H.A. Roberts, secretary to the Cambridge University Appointments Board
Construction:	External walls: 9in brickwork generally, 13½in on three-storey bale-end walls, with external render and limewash. Windows: painted softwood frames with oak sills, metal opening lights.
Roof:	Red clay plain tiles – at least three different sources used on original roof.
Present condition:	Very good after extensive repairs and re-roofing in 1990–91.
Garden:	Original layout still exists and is being restored and replanted.
Records:	Original byelaw application drawings in Cambridge City Guildhall.
Publication:	Baillie Scott & Beresford (1933) *Houses and Gardens,* and the *Architects' Journal,* 22 July 1992.

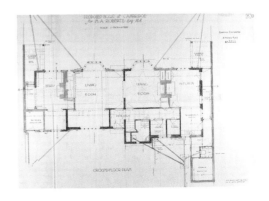

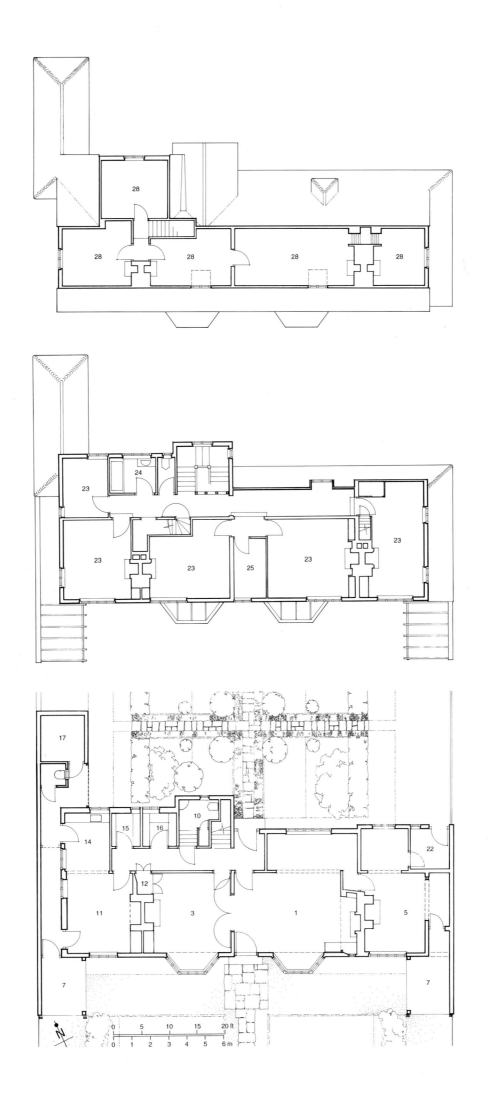

Landhaus Waldbühl

Location:	Uzwil, Switzerland
Date:	1907–11. Scheme design 1907–summer 1908; construction drawings 1908–09; construction May 1909–November 1911.
Client:	Theodor Bühler (1877–1915)
Construction:	External walls: masonry – tufa from northern Italy, with some timber-framing. Windows: timber-framed. Heating: original central heating installation still in use.
Roof:	Red clay tiles.
Present condition:	Excellent and original.
Garden:	Plans for entire property were made by Baillie Scott in 1910, but only the portion on the south of the house was carried out. Design includes a swimming pool and changing pavilion.
Records:	Complete records of drawings, correspondence and accounts retained by Bühler family.
Publication:	Katharina Medici-Mall (1979), *Das Landhaus Waldbühl: ein Gesamtkunstwerk zwischen Neugotik und Jugendstil.*
Notes:	Baillie Scott's commission was for a total decorative scheme, including furniture.

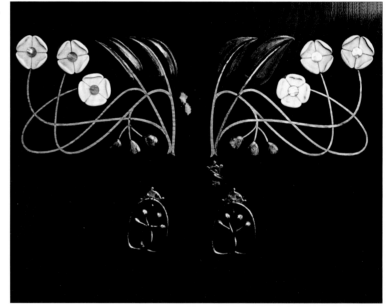

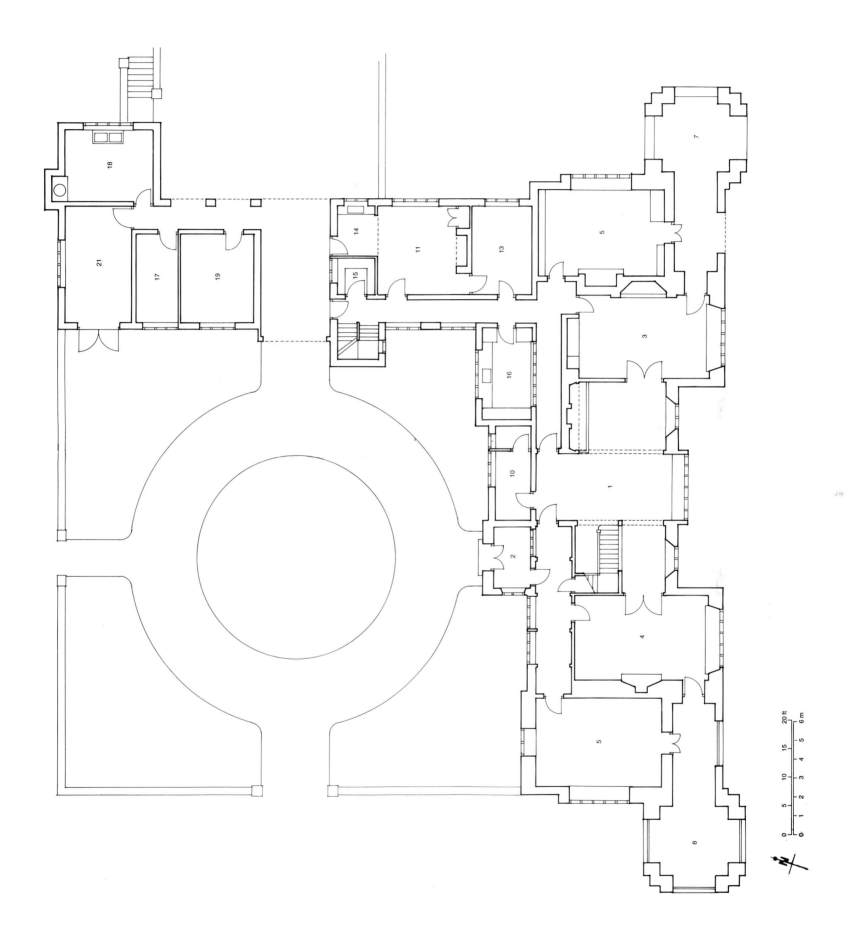

Church Rate Corner

Location:	Malting Lane, Cambridge
Date:	1924
Client:	Mrs Sewell, the builder was E.C. Northfield & Sons.
Construction:	External walls: cavity brick walls, hard external cement render with ochre limewash. Windows: oak-framed. Plasterwork: textured plaster. Heating: original installation still in use.
Roof:	Buff clay plain tiles.
Present condition:	Extensive repairs and re-roofing in 1992. New kitchen and bathroom.
Garden:	Original layout uncertain – Baillie Scott is not thought to have prepared a design.
Records:	No drawings remain.
Publication:	Never published.
Notes:	The house was built in the garden of an older house and is almost completely hidden, with a very modest entrance. It is a revelation, showing that Baillie Scott continued to refine the qualities of restraint and clarity in his later work. The planning, however, lacks the openness of many earlier houses.

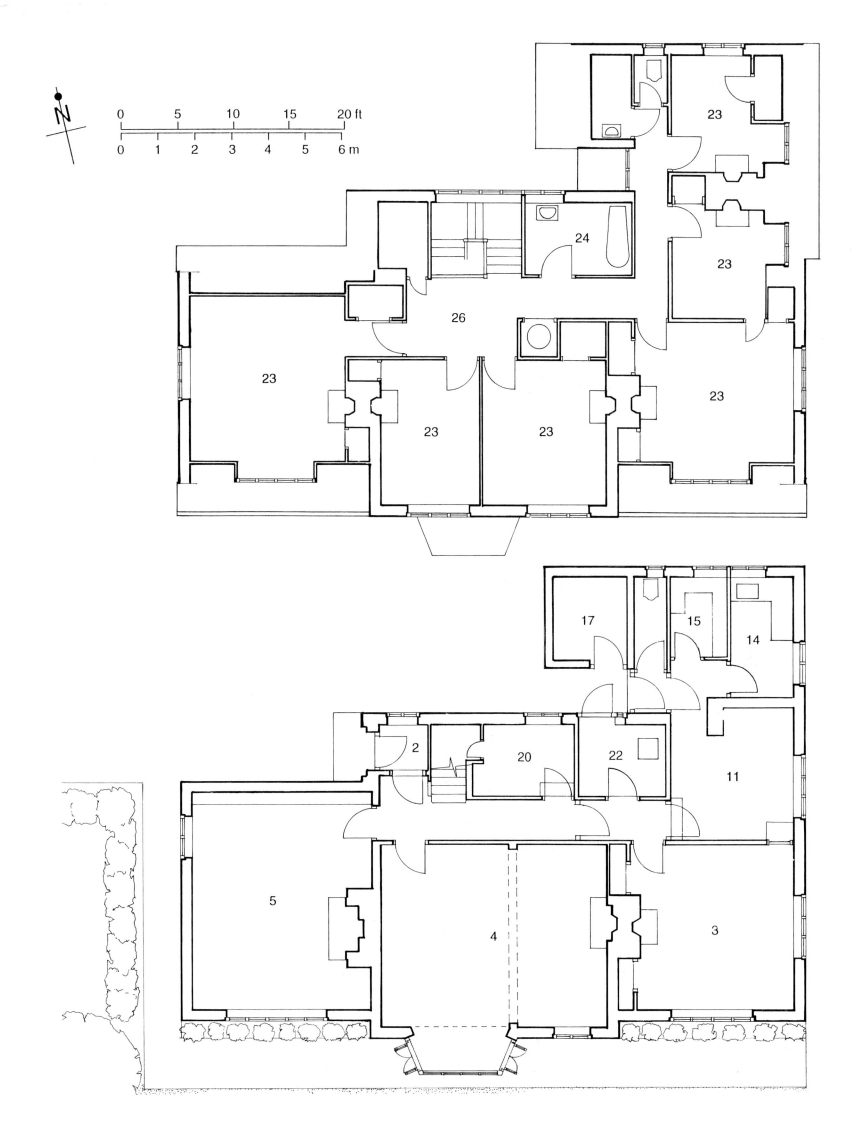

Mackay Hugh Baillie Scott
by John Betjeman

Drawing by Baillie Scott of the interior of Ockhams in Kent.

This is a personal reminiscence of one who, as a young man, knew Baillie Scott in the last years of his life. His life and works are being thoroughly annotated and catalogued by an American art-historian, Mr Kornwolf. This is fortunate since Baillie Scott's houses are numerous and unchronicled, his fabrics and wallpapers are out of print and his furniture and metalwork were so long out of fashion through the jazzy 1920s and serious 1930s that they are now very rare. Moreover some of his most spectacular designs to be found in the colour plates of the two books he published of his houses and gardens were never built. Baillie Scott's partner Beresford died in Newquay not long after his master, and the papers of the firm have disappeared.

I first came to know Baillie Scott when I was an assistant editor of the *Architectural Review* which was nominally edited by Christian Barman but really run and controlled by H. de C. Hastings of the Architectural Press. Those who thought they were advanced in 1930 despised what was called 'bankers' Georgian' just as we today despise 'bankers' functional'. Yet the *Architectural Review* could not quite throw off classical town halls and civic centres partly because of the advertising revenue that came from makers of bronze doors, light fittings and from importers of marble and stone. The only classical architect we were allowed to admire was Sir Edwin Lutyens. This was because he had in his youth been associated with the Arts and Crafts movement. We all knew, of course, that this movement was laughably out of touch with the great machine age into which we were emerging, but we realised that it was at least 'sincere' and not copying Greek and Roman details. And anyhow Lutyens was a rebel. Hadn't he had a row with the RIBA?

The new policy of the *Architectural Review* – or 'Architectural Revue' as Baillie Scott used to write it on his envelopes to me – was modern as opposed to *moderne*. We didn't like Cubism but we liked what was pure and simple and Scandinavian like our nominal editor. Edward and Prudence Maufe, the Mansard Gallery at Heal's and Carter's Poole Pottery were ousting the neo-Renaissance. Marble, bronze and gold were out, pastel shades were in. There had already been a Swedish number of the *Review* and Finland was leaping to the fore with the work of Alvar Aalto introduced by P. Morton Shand and J. Craven ('Plywood') Pritchard.

Frederick Etchells who had worked in the Omega workshops with Roger Fry had just translated Le Corbusier and designed the Crawford's building in Holborn, the first consciously functional building in London, the bare bones of its structure, concrete and steel boldly declaring themselves to the street. Peter Jones was beginning to show its starkness to Sloane Square. The architectural equivalents of Auden, Spender and Day Lewis were Serge Chermayeff, Wells Coates and Raymond McGrath. Their work filled the pages of the *Review* and in the new BBC building in Portland Place there was an uneasy alliance of these three with the Maufes, Eric Gill, and the bewildered architect of the building itself, Colonel Val Meyer, who was more used to designing blocks of flats.

When Hitler was starting in Germany, the architects of the Bauhaus came to England and were warmly welcomed and taken into partnership by the young functionalists. The Art-historians had slightly preceded them. Architecture was now solemn and moral. Decoration was wicked. We must look for sincerity, sources and roots. To be left was to be sincere. To be right was to be insincere. I think I believed this myself. We were sent thumbing through the early numbers of *The Studio* in search of our heritage of sincerity and socialism in the Arts and Crafts movement of 1890 onwards.

This was my introduction to Baillie Scott. This was the mood in which I approached the gods of the past. The first one to appear was C.F.A. Voysey who wrote a letter of protest against the modern format we had introduced into the *Review* – 'every page must be a surprise' said H. de C. It was...

Before introducing Baillie Scott, I must mention Voysey whose architecture bore a certain resemblance to the early Baillie Scott's work. They both liked sloping buttresses, pebble-dash and picturesque chimneys. They both had their work illustrated in *The Studio*. These two delightful men were complete contrasts as personalities and to describe Voysey helps me to picture Baillie Scott. They knew one another, but not well. When I once asked them both to lunch to meet, it was Baillie Scott who said that his early work had been influenced by Voysey.

Voysey was small, clean-shaven and bird-like. He wore black suits and his coats had no cuffs or lapels to them, as he considered these non-functional survivals of eighteenth-century foppery. He wore saxe blue shirts and a blue tie in a gold ring. He smoked a clay pipe. Daily he walked up St James' to sit in the Arts Club and drink sherry and argue. He was stimulating, decided, and not at all left wing. He disliked Morris 'because he was an atheist'. He himself was a theist and a follower of his father, the Reverend Charles Voysey, an Anglican clergyman of advanced theological views who left the Church of England to found the Theistic Church in Swallow Street. Voysey prided himself on being descended from John Wesley and had sat to Frank O. Salisbury for that artist's portrait of Wesley. The work of architects and artists which he did not admire and which one would have thought he might have admired, such men as Dawber and Munnings, he considered too 'peasant-like'. He thought Norman Shaw debased his genius by designing in the classical style. Gothic was the only style admired and the only living architect he admired was Comper whom he had never met. I arranged a little dinner party for Comper, John Summerson and Voysey. It was not the success we had hoped. Comper talked a lot. Voysey who liked talking hardly got a word in. I came across Voysey's letter of thanks in which he said 'What a pity Comper did not allow you to talk more.' ... This account of Voysey may make him sound crotchety and cantankerous whereas in truth he was a generous, humorous and a fundamentally modest man. His wife lived in their house, The Orchards, Chorley Wood, but Voysey preferred living in London and frequenting the Arts Club. Though he liked nature and based his decorative designs on flowers, birds and animals, he was really a town man and preferred human company even to nature. He mistrusted modern inventions like the cinema. His nephew, Robert Donat, took him to see Robin Hood at the London Pavilion in which Donat starred, 'Uncle Charles said "Take me out, take me out. I can't stand that screen with those faces twenty times life-size."' Voysey disliked all forms of distortion and he regarded his being thought a modern architect a distortion of the truth. He thought he was logically traditional.

Baillie Scott is far less easy to describe clearly. He was retiring, yet all-pervading. I wrote to him in his office in Bedford Row and was politely received by his partner, Beresford, who had at one time been chief assistant. There was no sign of Baillie Scott. He was in the country. Did I want to illustrate some of their houses in the *Review*? No, that was not really why I had come. I wanted to look at the early work. The houses he was building then (1931) seemed to be neo-Georgian and, though I did not say it, I would not have dared show such a style of house to H. de C. Hastings.

Later I had an invitation in a neat small hand on grey paper from Baillie Scott to come down and stay with him and his wife at their house, Ockhams, near Edenbridge, Kent. I must have made a favourable impression on Beresford. Ockhams was a Kentish farm house with an uneven tiled roof, brick chimney stacks, timbers and, as far as I remember, leaded windows but leaded, of course, in the right way, that is to say in oblong panes proportioned to the house. Any repairs and additions Baillie Scott had made were so subtly done that they looked as though they had always been there. Inside there was dark oak furniture, beaten copper, Regency furniture, watercolours and chintzes, but the chief thing I remember was the presence of flowers everywhere in patterns, in vases and where- ever you looked from the windows. Baillie Scott had designed the garden to provide small vistas from the house and when you were outside in the garden the old house seemed to grow out of flowers and shrubs and there was, of course, a background of oaks and elms.

I had been used to architects looking like architects. There were two types in the 1930s, the business man with a pin-striped suit and the addition either of an eyeglass or a little beard to show there was something artistic about him too, and there were the younger architects in hairy tweeds and knitted, woollen ties and bright shirts in primary colours. Baillie Scott was like neither type. He was an unassuming countryman and looked more like Thomas Hardy but bigger. He came of a 'landed' family and he had been intended by his parents for land agency work and to go out, when he had qualified, to Australia to manage large family estates there. He therefore went when he had left school to Cirencester College where he passed all his examinations and proudly kept the certificates for the rest of his life. This agricultural training must have given Baillie Scott his interest in trees and gardens which were always a part of his designs for houses.

He was never explicit about why he did what. He just took things as they came or as they struck his fancy. Thus we shall never quite know what made him chuck up Australia and go into the office of a Bath Architect named Davis who was responsible for the Empire Hotel in that city, although his marriage at that time may have had something to do with it. In his sleepy, laconic way with his melancholy expression, half-shut eyes and drooping moustache, Baillie Scott would simply say what had happened. 'I went to the Isle of Man for a holiday. I was so seasick I couldn't face the journey back so I set up in practice there. I was very advanced in those days. I remember I did some big designs for flower patterns and stained glass. There was an exhibition of them in Douglas. I didn't hang them myself and when I came to the exhibition quite a lot of them had been hung upside down. I thought they looked better like that.'

One of his early jobs in the Island was to supervise for J. L. Pearson the mosaic pavements in the chancel of St Matthew's, Douglas. It was about his only church work. Perhaps it was there that he met Archie Knox who was a worshipper at St Matthew's. They certainly knew each other, for Baillie Scott's daughter, Mrs Wallis, has some Archie Knox metalwork and remembers that he worked on designs in Baillie Scott's office and was associated with him in a Manx guild of craftsmen. There is no doubt that the range of colour in Knox's painting and the free style of his designs for Liberty's are similar to Baillie Scott's. When he left the Island Baillie Scott was presented with a silver box by the friends he had made there and this box is not at all art nouveau but just the usual thing in which freedoms of cities or cigars are put. Thus he must have known both the artists and more well-to-do people of the Island.

He was always very interested in craftsmen, particularly joiners and blacksmiths. The last letter he wrote to me shortly before he died was about a blacksmith of talent he had discovered in a village where he was staying near Torquay. When he left the Island he went straight to Bedford where he made designs for furniture carried out at the Pyghtle works there. In those early days, he said, advanced architects in London like himself always ate in Slater's tea shops. This was a matter of principle because the tea shops with their huge, circular entrances of bent glass and their swirling staircases within, were in an art nouveau style of which the young Baillie Scott approved more than Voysey would have done. I don't think any of these shops survive though many of us can remember them.

At Glencrutchery, outside Douglas, Baillie Scott did a job of interior decoration, stained glass, flock papers, light fittings and built-in furniture which was two years ago still surviving and which I hope is still there. With its pale green and violet and white – green and violet were the suffragettes' colours – it was the most complete art nouveau-cum-Morris interior I have seen. It was clearly on the Island that Baillie Scott got his inspiration for brilliant decorative colour contrasts which later made him famous throughout Europe when his drawings were reproduced in *The Studio*. He won a competition which Mackintosh also entered for a design for a house in the trees for a Queen of Romania… A great patron of the new art (Jugendstil) at the beginning of this century was the Prince of Hesse whose palace was in Darmstadt. Baillie Scott was sent for and met at the station by the royal carriage. Behind it was a wagonette with four horses for his luggage. This consisted of a single grip.

It was not as a decorator chiefly that Baillie Scott thought of himself. Architecture, that is to say, construction, the use of materials, plan and proportion mattered to him as much as 'delighte'. The police station which he built outside Castle Rushen, Castletown is an example of this. It is of local stone severely simple. It fits in with the grim castle and the little cottages and houses of the town as well. He much enjoyed building in different places traditional houses and cottages which could not be distinguished externally from those that had been in the district for centuries. Before 1914 and even after the First World War he was able to find local builders, slaters, thatchers and plasterers who could build in the style of their region. His cottages can be seen in most southern countries from Cornwall to Kent. It was his proudest boast, except that he never did boast and was never at all proud, that someone had written of his work 'he has built more houses that have done less harm to the landscape than any living architect'. When I told this to a member of the Modern Architectural Research Group to which I belonged in the 1930s he thought it merely comic because architecture should assert the machine age. Of course, in those days we thought that an international style was going to emerge that would fit in anywhere just as the stucco boxes of the Regency had done. Baillie Scott wrote to me that these architects who put up buildings which did not seem to have visible means of support, did not seem to have visible means of support themselves. Towards the end of his life Beresford, Baillie Scott and his son-in-law D. L. Wallis, who was a contractor, built many houses in a plain Georgian style, mostly of brick. This was because the men who could build in the old regional manner had disappeared and their skill and materials with them. The building that Baillie Scott told me he liked more than most he had built was the block of flats, Waterlow Court, in Hampstead Garden Suburb.

I said that Baillie Scott was retiring yet pervading. He was happiest in the country, an adored husband, father and grandfather, the comfortable centre of his hospitable world. Into that he received me, an unknown young man with no qualifications but in a sort of journalism with which he cannot be expected to have had much sympathy. He used to come up to London and stay with his wife at Kensington Palace Mansions Hotel, which he owned, and there I used to come and talk and laugh with them. After Mrs Baillie Scott died he went to Cornwall and then to Brighton and then came that last letter about the local blacksmith. In 1945, when he was dying, his daughter Mrs Wallis had a vision of very brilliant colours passing before her eyes, which were the colours he liked and which made him seem to her a being of colour. After his death life was emptier.

From The Journal of the Manx Museum, *vol. VII, no. 84, 1968. Reprinted here with kind permission of the Manx Museum.*

Memories of the Master

An interview with James Kennedy-Hawkes, FRIBA, who was an articled pupil with Baillie Scott and Beresford from 1928 to 1931.

Diane Haigh   You are the first person I've met who actually worked with Baillie Scott. I'd like to record your recollections so that others may share them.

James Kennedy-Hawkes   I was only fifteen-years-old when I was articled to Baillie Scott by my father, who was an able but modest architect in private practice. In many ways I would have preferred to continue my education at school – I missed the company of boys my own age – but in those days one didn't argue! In any case, my father was overjoyed at the opportunity for me to train with someone whom he greatly admired.

DH   Where was the office at that time?

JKH   When I started work, Baillie Scott and his partner Edgar Beresford had a small office at 8 Gray's Inn Square in London. Soon after, they moved a short distance to 29 John Street, Bedford Row. This was a bigger space, with room for me to have a drawing board of my own. The board lay on a bench raised at the rear on a stock brick, and I had a high stool to sit on. I remember how proud I felt, at fifteen, to be handling a loose T-square and professional instruments.

DH   What sort of work did you do as office junior?

JKH   Maurice Evans, the chief assistant, patiently taught me how to secure and release the drawing paper with brass pins, how to draw lines to scale with pen and pencil, and how to apply watercolour washes without damaging the paper. The junior often had to trace drawings: indeed, I traced many of the plans for the book of the partnership's work which was published in 1933.
   I had the opportunity to study all the drawings and documents that were sent out of the office, and later on to produce detailed drawings of all types of windows, doors, dormers and eaves, as well as alternative layouts of kitchens and bathrooms. I was sent out once a week to observe and report on works in progress, and later on to instruct and supervise them.

DH   Did you see much of the partners?

JKH   At that time Baillie Scott was sixty-three and Beresford forty-eight. As the new junior, the most contact I had was the occasional encouragement. The partners shared a separate room: they also seemed to share a sense of humour, for they would regale us with amusing anecdotes about their work.

DH   What sort of a person was Baillie Scott?

OPPOSITE: Sketches made by Baillie Scott for a house at Guildford, Surrey. The design dates from the early 1930s.

JKH   He seemed to be a very gentle man who enjoyed his work. He had an air of amusement about him: he liked cats and would doodle little sketches of them on the margins of his drawings. He was always beautifully dressed, usually in an astrakhan coat with a bowler hat and umbrella. He gave the impression of affluence – he lived at Kensington Palace Mansions Hotel during the week, and took taxis everywhere. I never met his wife but she had the reputation in the office of being quite a tartar who would keep him in line. None of the family ever came to the office.

DH   *Could you distinguish between the work of the two partners?*

JKH   Baillie Scott's work was usually identified by a very free plan. He worked as you should, from inside to out, and thought first about the internal spaces and their arrangement on plan. The resulting massing tended to be quite loose – often with a many-gabled garden frontage and bays under the eaves-overhang, and an irregular grouping of the kitchen offices to create an entry courtyard. Beresford's work, on the other hand, was tighter and more rectangular under a simple roof, and often more symmetrical. Beresford provided the working drawings for many smaller contracts: I am sure he was responsible for the Gate House at Limpsfield and for Ashwood at Woking, for example.

DH   *How was the office organised during your time there?*

JKH   The chief assistant was a crucial figure, acting as chief draughtsman and interpreter of the partners' sketches. In my time Maurice Evans filled that role, but it had been A.P. Starkey just before him. Baillie Scott would rough out his ideas in dimensioned plans and three-dimensional sketches and then hand over the design to Maurice Evans to set out, sort out the drains, and so on. The partners were the only ones who talked to the clients. Whilst I was in the office there were several other assistants, including John Street and R.P. Sharman. Letters were written in longhand and sent out to a copy-typing agency nearby. Specifications might also be typed or written in longhand in a duplicate book. Instructions to contractors were sent out on detailed drawings, dyeline-printed and watercoloured.

DH   *What sort of work were they doing during this period?*

JKH   There was Ashwood, the great house for Thomas Derry of Derry and Thoms. I remember Beresford provided Bills of Quantities with beautiful annotated sketches of all the details: the woodwork, designs for plaster ceilings by J.C. Pocock, etc. I also remember a house for Miss Cawthra, overlooking the tennis courts at Wimbledon. This was a direct copy of an old house in Kent: it had great timber beams which started to move and make loud popping noises when they turned on the heating! Another – uncharacteristic – aspect of the partnership's work were the houses they designed in places like Esher and Sevenoaks for Dudley Wallis [Baillie Scott's son-in-law, a building contractor]. They would produce just one sheet of drawings giving plans, elevations and the odd detail for a house on a one-acre plot. This was an unsatisfactory arrangement, as Wallis would make changes without consulting the partners, but times were getting hard in the 1930s and they were glad to have the work.

DH   *Were you involved in detailing any of these buildings? Were the details standard or reworked for each job?*

JKH   Baillie Scott was engaged in a crusade to revive and continue the crafts. He took great interest in how his houses were built. Bricks came from the Kent brickyards, usually made with a 1:1:6 mortar mix. Ironmongery would be produced by the local blacksmith to his designs. Windows came from Welstead Windows – each metal light was 1ft 8in wide whether it was fixed or opening. J.C. Pocock usually did the decorative plasterwork,.

I remember Baillie Scott was very upset by a new Buildings Byelaw which stipulated a minumum ceiling height of 8ft, as he felt this destroyed the low proportions of houses. He read a paper to the RIBA which led, among other revisions, to a new minimum of 7ft 6ins.

DH   Did you see much of other architects of that generation in the office?

JKH   The partners tended not to fraternise very much with other architects. However, Mr Martin-Kaye [son of Alex Koch] of *Architecture Illustrated* and W.J. Wills of the *Builder* were frequent visitors. These magazines – and *The Studio* – came into the office, but they were generally not kept, not even when they included the partners' own work.

DH   Why did you leave the practice?

JKH   By the time I finished my articles in 1931, the financial crisis was severely restricting the practice's output, so they had to let me go. Mr Baillie Scott wrote a very generous reference for me, which is now in the RIBA Library – dare I tell you – in the 'James Kennedy-Hawkes File', along with all the articles about the partnership kept by my father, who greatly admired their work.

This interview was held at the Royal Institute of British Architects in London in October 1994.

Advice for Baillie Scott House-Owners

Several owners have asked for advice on how best to care for Baillie Scott houses which are in need of repair work. Having been involved as an architect in the renovation of several Baillie Scott houses, it may be helpful to pass on observations from that experience. Many houses share the same problems: after all they are all now at least sixty years old, and some have already passed their century. They have become buildings of historical importance, and several have been recognised as such by being listed; these require Listed Buildings consent from planning authorities before any repair work can be carried out. But, whether listed or not, they have to be treated carefully by workmen familiar with traditional construction and by professionals competent to work with historic buildings.

SOUL OF THE BUILDING

Baillie Scott wrote about a mystic ingredient, 'a spirit of repose', to be found in his work. There is a particular atmosphere which you may recognise in your own house, but it is fragile and can be too easily covered up by layers of gloss paint, fitted carpets, plate-glass windows and too much furniture. Baillie Scott's own sketches show simple and uncluttered spaces. This simplicity is based in Arts and Crafts ideals and it is always how he pictured his houses. You may feel that you don't share that way of life – Mrs Baillie Scott didn't either and in her sitting room she had carpets and crystal chandeliers. But it was his vision that created the houses, and if you look carefully you may find overlooked elements which can be coaxed back to life: oak boarding under layers of paint, a fireplace long blocked up, an inglenook settle at the end of the garden. Look first for what is there in the quality of the house and take care of it, because that 'spirit' is so easily lost in sparkling new renovation work.

REPAIRS

1. Most Baillie Scott houses were built using very traditional construction – load-bearing masonry walls and timber-framed roofs. Generally, good quality materials were used and workmanship was to a high standard, all of which means they wear quite well. Repair work on the whole should be aimed at putting right specific defects that have arisen, piecing in new timbers, replacing tiles, etc., rather than wholesale renewal and modernisation.

2. Often the materials were chosen very specifically to give texture to the building and you may have found it difficult to get repairs to match with the existing. In replastering work, for example, there is no chance that modern plaster will be able to patch up a textured Baillie Scott plaster. The only way to achieve a successful repair is to analyse the original mix, which may well contain sharp and lime, and replicate it exactly. The plasterer should then lay it off with an old wooden float so that the material and the process – and consequently the result – are the same as the original.

3. Some houses are now facing fairly major repairs such as reroofing. It is critical to reroof with tiles that closely match the originals. Often a proportion can be saved from the

existing roof and additional sound second-hand tiles found to make up the remainder. But keep the texture and clay the same as the original roof – completely regular clay tiles (let alone concrete!) would spoil any Baillie Scott house. Roof insulation can be inserted when the covering is removed, but care should be taken to maintain good ventilation to the roof timbers. Gutters and downpipes were always in cast iron and should be replaced in the same material.

4. Structural problems sometimes arise from Baillie Scott's use of oak as structural timbers: posts, beams and joists. Oak is liable to move, sometimes pulling joists out of their bearings or more often sagging gradually over time and causing cracks. Timber members can be assisted by the judicious insertion of metal connectors or reinforcement, often in stainless steel, to stabilise the structure and prevent any risk of collapse.

5. Decoration is extremely important to the feel of an interior. Before 1900 Baillie Scott designed quite elaborate internal schemes, but after that date he recommended plain colours on the walls and never used wallpaper. It is often possible to tell what the original colour has been by lifting off a flake of paint back to the plaster and looking at the bottom layer. This would usually have been distemper, which gives a soft matt finish. It is still possible to redecorate with distemper, or alternatively to use a modern equivalent (for example, from the National Trust range). The right paint makes a big difference to the feel of a room. Oak boarding, doors or window sills would have been polished with beeswax polish and not painted, whereas softwood would most probably have been painted originally. External render, if painted at all, would have been limewashed, giving a much softer finish than modern external masonry paints. Most importantly, limewash also allowed the walls to breathe rather than creating a waterproof surface layer. It is a disastrous policy to apply impervious finishes over traditional materials, over stone mullions or roof finishes which were intended to get wet and then to dry out.

ALTERATIONS AND IMPROVEMENTS

6. Many alterations are undertaken to upgrade ancient services to meet modern expectations. Most Baillie Scott houses now have new kitchens and bathrooms. Even here thought can be given to fitting in sympathetically with the existing, rather than assuming a standard pattern of fitted kitchen. Most houses originally had both a scullery and kitchen. The scullery might still be the right place for the sink and fitted units, freeing the kitchen for the traditional working table. Cooking would originally have been on a solid fuel stove in the kitchen and that can be replaced by a modern stove. Storage would have been in a fitted dresser, some of which still survive.

Originally one bathroom was the norm for an average household, whereas we now generally expect more. In many houses there were small dressing rooms: the modern equivalent would include a shower. These small rooms can sometimes be usefully updated as bathroom accommodation without having to alter the plan. But Baillie Scott tried to organise his plumbing clearly, so look out for the logic behind the existing drainage stacks.

7. Heating and wiring installations have generally been superseded. When installing new service systems, it is crucial to formulate a strategy for conducting pipework or wiring which will minimise the need for breaking holes in the fabric of the building. Most houses have raised floors and attic spaces and a routing for pipework can often be devised, before work starts, to make use of these voids and reduce the visibility and destruction caused by the new services.

8. Modern levels of heating and lighting provision are far higher than in Baillie Scott's day. Just as he advocated 'practical and scientific ways of doing things', we should look to achieve new standards in clearly new, straightforward ways. Simple modern light fittings and radiators, if carefully designed, are often more successfully integrated than elaborate repro fittings, which are equally clearly not original. Sometimes lighting can be concealed in inglenooks, etc. to reduce the visible evidence of an installation.

9. Several householders have complained that their houses are very cold, not least because of the 9in brick solid external walls. It is important and relatively easy to install roof insulation, but much harder to insulate external walls: internal lining tends to put sills and skirtings in the wrong plane. There are other possible causes of heat loss. First, check draughtproofing around windows and doors and under floors. Second, check whether heat is being lost up chimneys. If not in use, these can be blocked off by inserting fireproof boards above the fireplace openings, although it is important to drill some large holes in the boards to allow trickle ventilation. Solid fuel stoves are far more efficient that large open fireplaces: they produce more heat from the fuel and their closed flues reduce heat losses up the chimney.

10. Many owners have experimented with double glazing. It is disastrous to remove the original leaded windows that are characteristic of Baillie Scott houses, still worse to also remove the mullions, and to replace them with new plate-glass lights. Baillie Scott said that it gave the house 'a blank and vacant stare', and it certainly destroys the original look. The most unobtrusive method of double-glazing seems to be to insert separate secondary windows internally between each mullion, which can be removable for cleaning or inward opening for ventilation.

Additions and Extensions

11. These are immensely difficult to achieve without swamping the original house. Several modest Baillie Scott houses have been totally overwhelmed by extensions completely out of scale with the original, both in height and breadth. Baillie Scott himself defended 'judicious and intelligent faking when dealing with old buildings' and felt that it was possible to add successfully if the new work is undertaken with 'the aim to achieve certain qualities of tone and workmanship belonging to old work'. This does not necessarily imply replication of the original construction, but certainly requires sensitive design thought about the scale and location of a new extension. One might check first that all attic and outbuilding space has been used up within the existing envelope.

12. The setting of several houses has also been irrevocably destroyed by the sale of the original large gardens. Bear in mind that the scale of a spacious house designed to sit in a garden is quite altered by bringing the boundary too close to the house, so that a bay window designed to give a broad view down the garden is now confronted immediately by a new boundary fence.

In the past many Baillie Scott houses have been unrecognised and badly treated and are now beyond redemption, which makes the survivors more precious and worthy of protection.

Chronology

- 1865 Born on 23 October, at Ramsgate, Kent. Childhood home at Worthing, Sussex.

- 1883 Enters Royal Agricultural College, Cirencester, Gloucestershire (October).

- 1885 Graduates with honours, Royal Agricultural College (December).

- 1886 Articled to Major Charles E. Davis, City Architect of Bath.

- 1889 Completes articles.
  Marries Florence Kate Nash (b. 1862) in Bath (February).
  Moves to Douglas, Isle of Man.
  Daughter born (November), Enid Maud Mackay Baillie Scott.

- 1891 Son born (May), Mackay Hugh Baillie Scott.
  First publication of 'Design for a Bungalow' in *Building News*.

- 1889–93 Architectural practice with Fred Saunderson, surveyor and land agent, at 7 Atholl Street, Douglas.

- 1892–3 Builds own house, the 'Red House', Douglas.

- 1893 Architectural practice from the Red House.

- 1895 First publication in *The Studio* (January): 'An Ideal Suburban House'.

- 1895 First commissions in England (Knutsford, Cheshire).

- 1896 First commission on the Continent (Belgium).

- 1897 Commissions in Darmstadt and Romania.

- 1901 Highest award in German competition 'Haus eines Kunstfreundes'. Moves to Bedford,

restoring 'The Manor' at Fenlake (one mile from Bedford). Publication of furniture designs in Pyghtle Works catalogue.

- 1903 Moves office from Bedford to 'The Manor', Fenlake.

- 1905 A. E. Beresford joins office as chief assistant.

- 1906 Publication of *Houses and Gardens*.

- 1911 'The Manor', Fenlake, destroyed by fire (March) – all records lost. Office moves to St John Street, Bedford; family moves to 'The Lodge', Elstow, near Bedford.

- 1912 Moves to flat in London; Beresford maintains office in Bedford.

- 1913–16 Moves to Haslemere, Surrey, and then to Farnham, Kent, and Bedford.

- 1914 Office closes for duration of First World War.

- 1916 Moves to the 'White House', Great Chart, Kent – extensive restoration work.

- 1919 Office re-opens as Baillie Scott and Beresford, at Gray's Inn, London.

- 1921 Moves to 'Ockhams', Edenbridge, Kent; maintains flat in Kensington Palace Hotel in London (owned by Scott family).

- 1927 Joins the Royal Institute of British Architects.

- 1930 Office moves to Bedford Row, London.

- 1933 Publication of second book, also called *Houses and Gardens* (joint author with Beresford).

- 1939 Death of Mrs Baillie Scott. Architectural practice closed.

- 1940/41 Office destroyed by bombing – all records lost.

- 1942 Sells 'Ockhams'; lives in rented cottages and nursing homes in Devon and Cornwall.

- 1945 Moves to nursing home in Brighton; dies on 10 February, aged 79.

Selected Bibliography

Books by M. H. Baillie Scott
• *Houses and Gardens* (1906)
London: Newnes
Translated into German as
Häuser und Gärten (1912)
Berlin: Wasmuth
• (With) A. E. Beresford (1933)
Houses and Gardens
London: Architecture Illustrated

Articles by M. H. Baillie Scott published in
The Studio
• 1895 'An Ideal Suburban House' (Jan.)
'The Decoration of the Suburban House' (Apr.)
'The Fireplace in the Suburban House' (Nov.)
• 1896 'An Artist's House' (Oct.)
• 1897 'On the Choice of Simple Furniture' (Apr.)
'A Small Country House' (Dec.)
• 1898 'Some Furniture for the New Palace,
Darmstadt' (July)
• 1899 'Decoration and Furniture for the New
Palace, Darmstadt' (Mar.)
• 1900 'A Country House' (Feb.)
• 1902 'A Country Cottage' (Apr.)
• 1903 'Yellowsands – A Seaside House' (Apr.)
'Some Experiments in Embroidery' (June)
• 1904 'A Cottage in the Country' (Aug.)
• 1905 'A House in Poland' (Jan.)
'A Hillside House' (May)
• 1906 June 'A House in the Midlands'
• 1907 'On the Characteristics of Mr C. F. A.
Voysey's Architecture' (Oct.)
• 1909 'Some Recent Designs of Mr M. H. Baillie
Scott' (May)
• 1912 'Some Recent Designs in Domestic
Architecture' (July)
• 1914 'A House in a Wood' (Jan.)
'The Cheap Cottage' (Mar.)

Selected Articles by M. H. Baillie Scott
• 'The Englishman's Home'
in Raymond Unwin et al (1909)
Town Planning and Modern Architecture in
Hampstead Garden Suburb, London
• 'Ideals in Building False and True'
in R. Weir Schulz (ed.) (1909)
The Arts Connected with Building
London: Batsford

• 'The Art of Building'
British Architect 28 January 1910
• 'The Making Habitable of Old Dwellings in
Town and Country'
RIBA Journal February 1919, pp. 73–81
• 'Texture'
The Architect 12 November 1926, pp. 551–2
Many of Baillie Scott's projects were published in
contemporary journals – see the Kornwolf mono-
graph for an extensive listing.

Contemporary Sources
• A. E. Beresford (1945)
'Architectural Reminiscences'
The Builder 10 August 1945, pp. 104–09
• Gertrude Jekyll and Lawrence Weaver (1912)
Gardens for Small Country Houses
London: Newnes
• Hermann Muthesius (1904)
Das Englische Haus (3 vols.)
Berlin
(Abridged English translation *The English House,*
1979, edited by Dennis Sharp)
• Barry Parker and Raymond Unwin (1901)
The Art of Building a Home: a collection of lectures
and illustrations
London: Longmans Green & Co.
• E. S. Prior (1901)
'Garden-Making' (three articles)
 The Studio October–December 1901
• John Dando Sedding (1891)
Garden-Craft Old and New
London: Kegan Paul, Trench, Trübner
• Raymond Unwin (1909)
Town Planning in Practice: an introduction to the
art of designing cities and suburbs
London and Leipzig: T. Fisher Unwin
• Raymond Unwin (1912)
Nothing Gained by Overcrowding: how the Garden
City type of development may benefit both the
owner and occupier
London: Garden Cities and Town Planning
Association

Modern Sources
• Isabelle Anscombe (1991)
Arts and Crafts Style
Oxford: Phaidon

• Clive Aslet
'Landhaus Waldbühl, Uzwil'
Country Life 17 January 1991, pp. 38–45
• Jane Brown (1982)
Gardens of a Golden Afternoon: the story of a
partnership – Edwin Lutyens and Gertrude Jekyll
London: Allen Lane
• Olive Cook and Edwin Smith (1954)
English Cottages and Farmhouses
London: Thames & Hudson
• Peter Davey (1980)
Architecture of the Arts and Crafts Movement
London: Architectural Press
(2nd edn. 1995, London: Phaidon)
• Stuart Durant (1992)
C. F. A. Voysey
London: Academy Editions
• Mark Girouard (1977)
Sweetness and Light: the 'Queen Anne'
movement 1860–1900
Oxford: Clarendon Press
• Trevor Graham (1993)
Melsetter House by William Lethaby
London: Phaidon
• A. Stuart Gray (1985)
Edwardian Architecture: a biographical dictionary
London: Duckworth
• Mary Greensted (1991; 1st edn. 1980)
Gimson and the Barnsleys
Stroud: Alan Sutton
• Diane Haigh (1992)
'M. H. Baillie Scott: 48 Storey's Way, Cambridge'
Architects' Journal 22 July 1992, pp. 26–39
• Dean Hawkes (ed.) (1986)
Modern Country Homes in England: the Arts and
Crafts architecture of Barry Parker
Cambridge: Cambridge University Press
• Wendy Hitchmough (1993)
'Lake Poetry'
Architectural Review December, pp. 72–8
• Edward Hollamby (1991)
The Red House by Philip Webb
London: Architecture Design and
Technology Press
• James D. Kornwolf (1972)
M. H. Baillie Scott and the Arts and Crafts
Movement: pioneers of modern design
Baltimore and London: Johns Hopkins Press

• Helen Long (1993)
The Edwardian House: the middle-class home in Britain 1880–1914
Manchester and New York: Manchester University Press
• Fiona MacCarthy (1994)
William Morris: a life for our time
London: Faber & Faber
• Robert Macleod (1971)
Style and Society: architectural ideology in Britain 1835–1914
London: RIBA Publications
• Katharina Medici-Mall (1979)
Das Landhaus Waldbühl von M. H. Baillie Scott: ein Gesamtkunstwerk zwischen Neugotik und Jugendstil
Bern: Gesellschaft für Schweiz. Kunstgeschichte

• Paul Oliver, Ian Davis, Ian Bentley (1981)
Dunroamin: the suburban semi and its enemies
London: Barrie & Jenkins
• David Ottewill (1989)
The Edwardian Garden
New Haven and London: Yale University Press
• Nikolaus Pevsner (1960; 1st edn. 1936)
Pioneers of Modern Design (original title *Pioneers of the Modern Movement*)
Harmondsworth: Pelican
• Nikolaus Pevsner (1968)
Art, Architecture and Design, vol. 2: Victorian and After
London: Thames & Hudson
• Margaret Richardson (1983)
Architects of the Arts and Crafts Movement
London: Trefoil Books

• Colin Rowe (1994)
The Architecture of Good Intentions: towards a possible retrospect
London: Academy Editions
• Paul Thompson (1967)
The Work of William Morris
London: William Heinemann
• Vincent Scully (1971)
The Shingle Style and the Stick Style (revised edn.)
New Haven and London: Yale University Press
• Alistair Service (1977)
Edwardian Architecture: a handboook to building design in Britain 1890–1914
London: Thames & Hudson

List of Works

This is primarily a list of projects mentioned in the text, and is not intended to be an exhaustive index. For the most thorough reference listing, see pp. 529–60 of the monograph by J. D. Kornwolf.

• 1892–3 The Mansion, later the Majestic Hotel, King Edward Road, Onchan, Isle of Man: Mr MacAndrew
• 1892–3 The Red House, Victoria Road, Douglas, Isle of Man: M. H. Baillie Scott
• 1893–4 Ivydene, Little Switzerland, Douglas, Isle of Man: Richard Maltby Broadbent
• 1893–4 Oakleigh, Glencrutchery Road, Douglas, Isle of Man: W. Macadam
• 1894–6 Bexton Croft, Toft Road, Knutsford, Cheshire: Donald MacPherson
• 1895–6 Holly Bank and Myrtle Bank, Victoria Road, Douglas, Isle of Man: W. Macadam
• 1895 Design for a House (not built), Bedford: Carl St Amory
• 1896–7 Leafield and Braeside, King Edward Road, Onchan, Isle of Man, Douglas Bay Estate Co.
• 1897–8 Dining and drawing rooms (destroyed), Ducal Palace, Darmstadt, Germany: Grand Duke Ernst Ludwig of Hesse
• 1897–8 Five Gables, 4 Grange Road, Cambridge
• 1897–8 Glencrutchery House interiors (dismantled), Douglas, Isle of Man: Deemster Thomas Kneen

• 1897–8 Terrace Houses, Falcon Cliff Terrace, Douglas, Isle of Man: W. Macadam
• 1897–8 Village Hall, Onchan, Isle of Man: Onchan Parish
• 1897 Design for a House, Brussels, Belgium: Willy Schlobach
• 1898–9 Blackwell, Windermere, Westmorland: Sir Edward Holt
• 1898–9 White Lodge, Wantage, Berkshire
• 1899–1900 White House, 5 Upper Colquhoun Street, Helensburgh, Scotland: H. S. Paul
• 1899–1900 Winscombe, Beacon Road, Crowborough, Sussex
• 1899–1901 Police Station, Castle Rushen, Castletown, Isle of Man
• 1901–1902 Fenlake Manor (renovation), Cardington Road, Fenlake, Bedford: M. H. Baillie Scott
• 1901 Dulce Domum (*Haus eines Kunstfreundes*) competition design
• 1903–04 House in Russia
• c. 1903–04, House in Switzerland: Alfred Bussweiler
• 1904 Heather Cottage, off Cross Road, Sunningdale, Berkshire
• 1904 The Crow's Nest (now The Dove's Nest), Ashdown Forest, Duddleswell, Sussex
• c. 1904–05 Elmwood Cottages, 7–7a Norton Way North, Letchworth, Herts: First Garden City Corporation

• 1905 The Haven, Leatherhead, Surrey
• 1905 Springwood, Spring Road, Letchworth, Herts: Edward Docker
• c. 1905 Coval Court, off Cross Road, Sunningdale, Berkshire
• before 1906 The Cloisters (not built)
• 1906–07 Bill House, Grafton Road, Selsey-on-Sea, Sussex: Byron Peters
• 1906–07 Tanglewood, 17 Sollershott West, Letchworth, Herts: Mrs Branson
• 1906–07 Green Place, Stockbridge, Hants: Mrs E. M. Hill
• c. 1906–09 Greenways, Devenish Road, Sunningdale, Berkshire: Earl of Lindsay
• 1907–08 Corrie Wood, Hitchin Road, Letchworth, Herts: J. S. Lamb
• 1907 House, 29 Norton Way, North Letchworth, Herts: S. W. Palmer
• 1907 Rake Manor (additions), Rake Lane, Milford, Surrey: Archdeacon Beresford Potter
• c. 1907 King's Close, Church Lane, Biddenham, Beds: Miss Steele
• 1907–11 Waldbühl, Uzwil, Switzerland: Theodor Bühler
• 1908–09 Burton Court and cottage Longburton, Sherborne, Dorset: E. W. Bartlett
• 1908–1909 Garden Court, Warwick's Bench, Guildford, Surrey
• 1908–09 Rosewall, Calonne Road, Wimbledon, Surrey

- 1908–09 Undershaw, Warwick's Bench, Guildford, Surrey: Mr Pimm
- 1908 Terrace houses, Meadway, Hampstead Garden Suburb
- 1908 White Cottage, Sudbury Hill, Harrow, Middlesex: Alfred Bussweiler (Boswell)
- 1909 Seal Hollow, Sevenoaks, Kent
- 1908–09 Waterlow Court, Heath Close, Hampstead Garden Suburb: Improved Industrial Dwellings Co.
- 1909 White Cottage, 17 Church End, Biddenham, Beds: Miss Street
- 1910–11 Pair of cottages, 36 and 38 Reed Pond Walk, Gidea Park: Gidea Park Development Co., Romford, Essex
- 1910 Home Close, Sibford Ferris, Oxfordshire: E. E. Borne
- 1911 Fox Hill Cottage, Haverhill Road, Stapleford, Cambs: Sir Harry Anderson
- 1911 The End House, Lady Margaret Road, Cambridge: J. F. Cameron
- 1912–13 House, 14 Western Drive, Short Hills, New Jersey: Henry Binsse
- 1912–13 House, Laskowicze, Witebsk, Poland: M. W. Chludzindski
- 1912–13 The Cloisters (demolished), Avenue Road, Regent's Park, London: Sir Boverton Redwood
- 1912–21 Pilgrims Chilham, Kent: Mr Sanderson
- 1912 Michaels (now Havisham House), Palmar's Cross Hill, Harbledown, Canterbury: Alfred Earl
- 1912–13 House, 48 Storey's Way, Cambridge: H. A. Roberts
- 1913 House, 144 Cooden Sea Road, Bexhill-on-Sea, Sussex: Sir Boverton Redwood

- 1914 Gyrt-Howe, 30 Storey's Way, Cambridge: J. M. Edmonds
- 1916–17 White House (restoration), The Street, Great Chart, Kent: M. H. Baillie Scott
- 1919–20 Buckleberry Grange, Buckleberry Common, near Reading, Berkshire
- 1919–20 The Tudors, South Park Crescent, Gerrard's Cross, Henderson, Bucks: J. Neal
- 1919–20 Westhall Hill, Burford, Oxfordshire: J. Kettlewell
- 1919 Restoration of seventeenth-century house, 8 Quarry Street, Guildford, Surrey: M. H. Baillie Scott
- 1920–21 Ockhams (restoration), off Marsh Green Rd, Edenbridge, Kent: M. H. Baillie Scott
- 1921–2 Two Ways, Old Mill Lane, Bray-on-Thames, Berkshire: Mr Sanderson
- 1922 Lennel, 54 Storey's Way, Cambridge: C. Wright
- 1922 Greenways, Kippington, Sevenoaks, Kent: Sir Guy Mottbower
- 1922 House, 29 Storey's Way, Cambridge: Reverend Dr E. H. Askwith
- 1922 Mere House, The Green, School Lane, Hamble, Hampshire: Captain Lubbock
- 1922 The Manor House (rebuilding), Little Bookham, Surrey
- 1923 Squerryes, 56 Storey's Way, Cambridge: G. E. T. Wilson
- 1923 The Gatehouse, Ballard's Way, Limpsfield, Surrey: Stanley Farr
- 1923 Three Elms, Kippington, Sevenoaks, Kent: D. L. Wallis
- 1924 Church, Rate Corner, Maltings Lane, Cambridge: Mrs Sewell
- 1924–5 Raspit Hill, Ivy Hatch, Ightham, Kent: Mrs Fraser

- 1924–7 New Hall, Bembridge School, Bembridge, Isle of Wight: J. H. Whitehouse
- 1924 Cory Lodge, University Botanical Gardens, Cambridge: Curator of University Botanical Gardens
- 1924 Thorndyke, Huntingdon Road, Cambridge: E. G. Ludlum
- 1925 House, 7 Constable Close, Hampstead Garden Suburb
- 1926–7 Snowshill Manor Garden, Snowshill, Broadway, Gloucestershire: Charles Wade
- 1926 Hadleigh, 138 Huntingdon Road, Cambridge: Professor Sir Frank Engledon
- 1928–9 Ashwood, Ashwood Road, Woking, Surrey: Thomas Derry
- 1928–9 Kilnwood, Barberries, Donyland Cottage, Sevenoaks, Kent: Messrs G. E. Wallis
- 1929 Witham, Woodland Rise, Seal, Kent: Messrs G. E. Wallis
- 1931–2 Cassey Barn, The Oaks, Cove Cottage, Ashley Drive, Walton-on-Thames, Surrey: Price & Brassey-Taylor
- 1931–2 Coval Copse, Sandy End, Arbourne, Esher, Surrey: Messrs G. E. Wallis Kirkby Underwood, The Woodlands, Low Wood, Caribou: Sandy Holt
- 1936–8 Clobb Copse, Buckler's Yard, High Street, Beaulieu, Hants: John Ehrmann